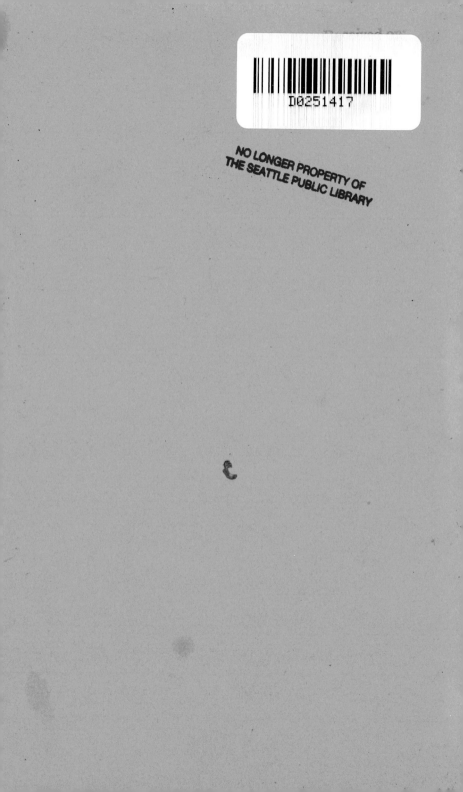

D0251417

"At midlife, we are forced to wrestle with the fundamental question of how to live authentically and make the most of life. In *40/40 Vision*, Greg Lafferty and Peter Greer provide biblical and practical insights on how to sort through such issues as busyness, unmet expectations, the pursuit of pleasure, wisdom, injustice and identity. Ultimately, they inspire us to lean into the future, seek our pleasure in God and learn to live redemptively. For those well into the race of life or ready for a fresh start, *40/40 Vision* is sure to be an energetic and welcome encouragement."
Ken Wytsma, author of *Pursuing Justice* and *The Grand Paradox*

"*40/40 Vision* is not just a book; it's also a mirror helping us reflect on the trajectory of our lives. As the psalmist tells us to number our days in order to gain wisdom, see this as a tool to help count. Through the lens of Ecclesiastes, Greer and Lafferty show us it's not a midlife crisis, but a midlife opportunity. If you're hungry to learn from the wisdom of others who have traveled—and who are currently traveling—life's path, this book is for you."
J.R. Briggs, pastor, author of *Fail* and coauthor of *Eldership and the Mission of God*

"Having recently turned forty, I'm grateful for how *40/40 Vision* provides a great opportunity to reflect on the past and look toward a meaningful future. We don't want this second half of life to slip by. We're invited to live it faithfully and fully—in how we love our families, serve in the world, do our work and seek God."
Kent Annan, author of *After Shock* and *Following Jesus Through the Eye of the Needle*

"I turned forty this year, and I'm happy to report, I'm still the same person I was last year . . . but not without a bit of existential angst about the brevity of life. In this timely book, Peter and Greg guide us to reflect on the gifts of growing older, inviting us to learn from past mistakes and refocus on what matters most. This is a book everyone in the midst of midlife needs to read."
Kristen Howerton, founder of Rage Against the Minivan

"With wisdom and vulnerability, Greer and Lafferty challenge us with questions that really matter—about our identity, our relationships, and our plans and purposes. *40/40 Vision* is a must-read for anyone wanting to more clearly see a life well lived!"
Tom Lin, InterVarsity vice president, director of Urbana, Lausanne Movement international deputy director

"Peter and Greg's book reminds me to look beyond life's repetitive and sometimes seemingly meaningless cycles, to the deepened, perspective-driven wisdom and productivity that awaits me on the other side of forty. The book weaves practical, real-life examples alongside some of the musings of Solomon from Ecclesiastes to engage the reader to reach for a higher world, in living 'above the sun,' no matter the life stage they are part of."
Sarah Cunningham, author of *The Well-Balanced World Changer* and *Portable Faith*

"The sobering realities of midlife may offer the most opportunity and risk for followers of Christ. During this time, the importance of our ability to thoughtfully reflect and respond to God's call to walk with him cannot be overstated. In *40/40 Vision*, Peter and Greg have written an honest and essential guidebook to help us navigate the rest of our days. It's a must-read."

Dave Blanchard, CEO and cofounder of Praxis

"As I approach my forties, I find myself thinking about what's next and assessing what I've done and have left to do. At a time when all of us at any age can find ourselves pondering our gifts, talents and callings, this book calls us to be hopeful through all seasons and believe that our best is yet to come, no matter our age. Just as Moses didn't start his most notable ministry until later in life, this book invites us to not waste our time thinking what could have been and focus instead on what could be."

Jenny Yang, vice president of advocacy and policy, World Relief, coauthor of *Welcoming the Stranger*

"As a forty-six-year-old dad with four sons, I can testify that midlife is a turbulent time. It's easy to lose our perspective and stumble at a time when our families need us most. Peter and Greg help us see clearly through the haze of midlife and live for what ultimately matters. I am grateful for their insights and confident you will be as well."

Scott C. Todd, senior vice president for global advocacy, Compassion International

"*40/40 Vision* is a trove of timeless wisdom and timely insight. It penetrates many blind spots of our own era as well as great questions asked throughout history. Ultimately, it points not only to hope on the far side of the forties but also to weighty purpose and a light heart within them."

Jedd Medefind, president, Christian Alliance for Orphans, coauthor of *Upended*

"This book came to me right as I was entering my forties. It had a profound impact on me, altering the way I will view this chapter of my life as well as the trajectory of my future. I am certain it will do the same for you!"

Robert Dickie, president of Crown Financial Ministries

40/40
VISION

CLARIFYING YOUR MISSION
IN MIDLIFE

PETER GREER AND GREG LAFFERTY
FOREWORD BY BOB BUFORD

IVP Books

An imprint of InterVarsity Press
Downers Grove, Illinois

InterVarsity Press
P.O. Box 1400, Downers Grove, IL 60515-1426
ivpress.com
email@ivpress.com

InterVarsity Press® is the book-publishing division of InterVarsity Christian Fellowship/USA®, a movement of students and faculty active on campus at hundreds of universities, colleges and schools of nursing in the United States of America, and a member movement of the International Fellowship of Evangelical Students. For information about local and regional activities, visit intervarsity.org.

While any stories in this book are true, some names and identifying information may have been changed to protect the privacy of individuals.

Published in association with the literary agency of Wolgemuth & Associates.

Cover design: David Fassett
Interior design: Beth McGill
Images: Exactostock/Superstock/Glow Images

ISBN 978-0-8308-4434-0 (print)
ISBN 978-0-8308-9888-6 (digital)

Printed in the United States of America ♾

Library of Congress Cataloging-in-Publication Data

Greer, Peter, 1975-
40-40 vision : clarifying your mission in midlife / Peter Greer and Greg Lafferty ; foreword by Bob Buford.
pages cm
ISBN 978-0-8308-4434-0 (hardcover : alk. paper)
1. Middle-aged persons—Religious life. 2. Vocation—Christianity. 3. Bible. Ecclesiastes—Criticism, interpretation, etc. I. Title. II. Title: Forty-forty vision.
BV4579.5.B33 2002
248.8'4—dc23

2015026990

P	20	19	18	17	16	15	14	13	12	11	10	9	8	7	6	5	4	3	2	1
Y	32	31	30	29	28	27	26	25	24	23	22	21	20	19	18	17	16	15		

To Keith and Bonnie Greer,
parents who encouraged me (Peter)
to look above the sun.

And to Deane,
who has stuck with me (Greg) through thick
and thin—mostly thick, assuming that's
the positive half of the phrase.

Of making many books there is no end.

ECCLESIASTES 12:12

CONTENTS

FOREWORD

Bob Buford

⤢

More than three decades have passed since my fortieth birthday, but that period in my life remains vivid in my memory.

It was a time when I suddenly found myself in a "success panic." I was the leader of a successful company, the husband of a woman I respected and loved, and the father of a beautiful son. I had everything that was supposed to make me happy. Yet gnawing questions haunted me: How could I experience such success, such blessings, while still feeling so unfulfilled? If success didn't fill my life with meaning, what would? In exploring these doubts, I entered into a long line of people who have looked at their life's work and wondered if there's any purpose in it.

At seventy-five years old, I now know without any doubt that resolution to these crucial questions is found in relationship with our Creator—the One in whom we live and move and breathe. That's been true for all time.

But the form that our response takes as we move beyond midlife changes from generation to generation. Part of the way forward for me, as I shared in my book *Halftime*, was finding a parallel career in which I could use my gifts to bring glory to God within my context.

As today's midlifers ask questions about how to live well in the second act of their lives, they face a unique set of challenges. This generation lives in a day marked by rapid technological advances, economic fluctuations, unprecedented numbers of depression diagnoses, increased globalization and the influence of postmodernism. Fortunately there are also new leaders rising up to help guide the conversation. Peter Greer and Greg Lafferty are two such leaders. And the conversation they initiate in this important and illuminating book reassures me that our younger generations are in good hands.

With boldness and humility, Greg and Peter scrutinize mortality—including their own—with inspired wisdom, keen insight and refreshing humor. Using the book of Ecclesiastes—a segment of Scripture that is often overlooked because it's so mystifying—as a guide, they bring fresh insight not only to biblical interpretation but also to age-old questions about existence and meaning.

Through this book, Peter and Greg speak to the importance of deep relationships and connection with others. At the same time, they model the kind of discipleship they prescribe. Their friendship, which comes to life in the pages of this book, demonstrates how those who have already walked the path can offer the support and care needed to navigate this uncertain period. That's where the unique power of this book lies.

And although this book is about midlife, it isn't just for middle-aged people. If you are, like me, an older man or woman, I encourage you to invite a younger person to read this book with you and to share your own story in the process.

If you are in your twenties or thirties and midlife still seems far off, I invite you to spend some time looking ahead with someone who's already journeyed through those years. As my friend Peter Drucker wrote, "There is one prerequisite for managing the second half of your life: You must begin long before you enter it."[1] Questions about meaning and significance confront us not just in midlife but throughout the course of our years, so the issues discussed in this book are relevant to just about everyone.

Like many in their generation, these coauthors have already involved themselves in significant endeavors: Peter as president of a sizable nonprofit, and Greg as the pastor of a flourishing church. Yet they are asking questions to position themselves for even more significance in their second half.

To navigate these years well, you must think about how to finish well. You can take my word for it: time vaporizes in the blink of an eye, so don't waste your life being impeded by blurry vision. Rather, press on with clarity and with focus, so that you not only run the race but also keep the faith.

INTRODUCTION

⤢⤡

Recently I (Peter) awoke to a simple reality: there is more of my life in the rearview mirror than out the windshield.

According to the World Health Organization, the average life expectancy for a person born in the United States is seventy-nine years.[1] Having recently celebrated my fortieth birthday, I'm more than halfway there. I don't need a cake full of candles to convince me of the brevity of life.

Not long ago, I was in Miragoane, Haiti, a couple of hours from Port-au-Prince, to spend time with the staff of HOPE International, a global microfinance ministry in which I serve. Nearing the conclusion of our trip, our small team was on its way back to the capital city when we came across a line of cars stopped at a roadblock. The community had been promised electricity, but it had never come. In protest, a group of upset men was blocking the road with two giant buses.

So we waited. And waited. There's not much of an alternative when you reach a roadblock in rural Haiti. As more minutes passed, we realized we were going to miss our flights—and the urgent priorities waiting for us back home—if we didn't find a creative way around this obstacle.

Eager to help, Vitol, our driver and guide, stepped out of the car and returned moments later with a local community member who promised that he knew the protesters and could navigate the blockade. The few dollars he required for his services seemed like a bargain.

Sitting in the driver's seat and laying on the horn, our new driver carefully wound around the buses in our way. But a hundred yards later, we faced a more difficult barrier. A truck with slashed tires was blocking the road. A car had attempted to squeeze past it but got stuck in the ditch, extending the blockade.

There was no way through.

Our driver turned down a side road paralleling the main one in an attempt to bypass the mess. After passing an eerily empty police station, we heard shouting and saw some of the protesters rushing toward us, obviously upset by our attempted workaround. The mob swirled around our car. Up ahead we saw a man pull a pistol from his pocket and cock it. Screaming in Creole, he rushed menacingly toward us.

I said something manly like, "Oh dear," and then we ducked and prayed.

After a heated discussion between the driver and the gun-waving protestor, we settled on a price and were able to continue on our way. A loaded gun is a powerful negotiating tool.

Shaken but unharmed, we made it back to the capital city and flew off. When I arrived home, I hugged my wife and kids longer than usual. Reminded of the shortness of life, for the next week I took every opportunity to make sure they knew how much I love them.

As if this event were insufficient to get my attention, four months later I was flying within the Democratic Republic of Congo on the only available airline, Mango Air, aboard an ancient Russian plane, the Antonov 26. (Note to self: always check make and model of aircraft before boarding.) The sketchy-looking machine was overloaded with cargo, primarily palm oil being transported from Kisangani to Bukavu.

As the heavy plane struggled to take off, it barely cleared the trees. We then flew over the Congolese jungle at an exceptionally low altitude and managed to land safely. Later we found out that just two weeks after our flight, the same plane on the same route had caught fire while landing, killing everyone on board. I mourned for the men and women we had been with just a short time earlier.

I am no adrenaline junkie, so these events had me thinking seriously about my own mortality for the first time. And now I find my fortyish body taking off slower, flying lower and landing harder than ever before. The decade that I'm entering isn't known for bliss and smooth sailing.

The December 2014 cover story in *The Atlantic* summarizes research showing the correlation between age and happiness. Life satisfaction steadily declines in the twenties and thirties, bottoms out in the forties, but then increases through the fifties, sixties and seventies. When plotted, this data looks like a U-curve reaching the lowest point right around the next mile marker on my road.[2]

This U-curve has gone global. In 2008, researchers conducted a global survey asking, "All things considered, how satisfied are you with your life as a whole these days?" In fifty-five of the eighty countries where they administered the survey, individuals in midlife were least satisfied, and the nadir was age forty-six.[3]

Correspondingly, in twenty-seven European countries, researchers identified a "strong hill-shaped pattern" in the use of antidepressants. The peak age of antidepressant use is the late forties, and the likelihood of using antidepressants "nearly doubles" during midlife.[4]

Most of us have seen dramatic midlife crashes fueled by discontent and perhaps participated in and experienced some of the damage ourselves. Seemingly out of the blue, friends or family members have had major lapses in judgment. Maybe we've committed a few ourselves. These decisions make no sense—but midlife is known for rashness, not rationality.

Consider the dad who has a beautiful home, wife and kids, then has an affair and loses everything he once held dear. Or the devoted mom who is emotionally crippled by the failures of her children. The business leader who achieves the highest level of success but is caught in a financial scandal and forced out in disgrace. The former prom queen who is consumed by her fight against aging. The single friend who never married and grows bitter and resentful. The pastor who diligently builds a congregation but burns out after years of neglecting his own soul.

Even if we don't experience a dramatic midlife crisis, there are still potential problems to avoid. In midlife we may grow bored with success or despair at our failures. We may feel trapped by marriage or hopeless in singleness. We may suffer our first big physical breakdown or watch a parent suffer their last one. As we head into the turbulence ahead, it's time to ensure our seat belts are securely fastened.

In 1965, Canadian psychologist Elliott Jaques created the term *midlife crisis* to describe the stress induced by looking one's mortality in the eye. [5] We realize our lives have an expiration date. "Forty is the old age of youth," as Victor Hugo famously wrote, "fifty the youth of old age."[6]

Many will say, "So be it. In the end, we die. So live it up. Indulge the desire. Have the fling. Pursue the thrill." But even as we give ourselves license, the agitation persists. Deep questions linger. We can't escape them.

But it's not all doom and gloom. Opening our eyes to our mortality and limitations can allow us to live more fully. Midlife is an opportunity to leave some of our youthful folly behind, to look back at our first forty and refocus on what matters most for our next forty—or however long we have. It's a time to prepare for our second act, to get our second wind.

After all, midlife is a test in the middle of *life*—not death—and it's an exam I desperately want to pass. Thankfully I don't have to do it alone.

My friendship with Greg began when I was thirty. I had just started a new job, moved to Lancaster, Pennsylvania, and become a first-time father. As a young leader with responsibilities better fitting someone beyond my age and experience, I knew I needed a mentor. As a pastor of a nearby vibrant church and as someone a decade ahead of me in years and experience, Greg helped me traverse my thirties, serving not only as a board member of HOPE International but also as a friend.

As I watched him, it was clear that he navigated his forties with resilience and, even more importantly, with unflinching honesty. Because of his humility in success and candor in failure, I respected how he led and learned. Now in his fifties, with his humor, faith and family intact, he is being shaped positively by this decade.

As one committed to understanding and applying Scripture, Greg studied the book of Ecclesiastes and used it as the lens to explore midlife—two seemingly depressing things—in a way that was hopeful, helpful and even enjoyable. Although midlife is never mentioned in Scripture, Greg showed that Ecclesiastes asks the key questions that an awareness of our mortality in midlife demands we answer. It is these questions we consider throughout this book.

Despite Greg's many other priorities in leading his church and ministries, I coerced him into this book project because I want to see clearly, serve faithfully, live generously and age gracefully. Because I understand that midlife is a strategic time to prepare for life's second act. Because I want to go beyond avoiding a midlife crisis and instead be propelled into meaningful mission. Because I want to risk everything for what ultimately matters. And because I want my friends and family to flourish through the years ahead.

Our hope is that this is not just another self-help book loosely based on Christian principles or a list of ways to ease the symptoms of midlife. Rather, we want to address the underlying questions of midlife through the timeless wisdom of Ecclesiastes. Although many face these issues in their forties, others face them in their thirties or fifties. The point is that we all must face significant questions about life and death that Ecclesiastes invites us to explore courageously.

If you hate this book, please email me. But if you find it helpful, please email Greg, for it is his work, experience and thinking that grounds this project in timeless biblical wisdom and practical application.

Thank you for joining the conversation, for taking a shot at finding new depths of meaning and contentment, and for working with us to preempt your own midlife crisis.

FORTY(ISH)

What's So Special About Forty?

*I believe the forties to be
dangerous, uncharted waters.*

GORDON MACDONALD

Turning forty stunk.

And since it did, let's start with thirty. I (Greg) was very happy to turn thirty.

The generation before mine lived by a well-known axiom: "Don't trust anyone over thirty." But as I came of age, I realized that the rest of the world was actually saying, "Don't trust anyone *under* thirty." If you're in your twenties, you're still a kid.

And I looked like one.

Every month I went to the barbershop, sometimes on my lunch break. The guy cutting my hair invariably asked, "No school today?" I guess I didn't look like the type to skip or like the type to have graduated. "Nope, no school today—or any day. I actually have a job," I'd say in a chipper voice.

I endured this dialogue for years. Then they finally broke me at age twenty-six. One day I went in for my customary haircut, but there was a new woman working, maybe in her midthirties. She was reasonably attractive and not much older than I was. We made small talk through the fifteen-minute procedure, and then I got up to pay. That's when she offered me a lollipop. A *sucker.* Is that what I looked like? I went to a different barber after that.

To make matters worse, I was a youth pastor, which to most people meant that I played with kids for a living. Guilt by association. And though I was married, Deane and I remained childless for quite a while, meaning we enjoyed none of the credibility that comes from being in the Parent Club.

But early in 1992, I turned thirty. What's more, Deane was pregnant. To top it off, the church let me preach my first sermon. *What say ye now, world?* I was an adult, a force to be reckoned with. My thirtieth birthday was a great celebration.

But when I turned forty, I felt none of that pride of passage. Rather, I felt dread and foreboding. I was suddenly old and supposedly mature.

I have a naturally buoyant personality, but I was blue and surly for all ten of my birthdays that started with a four. We joke about it now, but I made it almost impossible for my wife and kids to get the celebration right. Go big, and I didn't like it: "What's the big deal? It's just a number!" Downplay my birthday, and it was, "What? I'm just taken for granted around here?"

One year my wife swears that she and the kids got me a bunch of presents and I didn't like a single one. I don't remember that, but I can't deny that it *might* have happened. If it did, it was probably on my forty-sixth birthday, the typical low ebb of midlife self-loathing.

Forty Matters

In the Bible, forty plays a prominent and recurring role. It crops up everywhere. Many of the best-known stories have the number forty associated with them:

- It rained forty days on Noah.

- Moses spent forty years in Egypt, forty years in Midian and forty years post-Exodus. When he went up on Mt. Sinai, he stayed there forty days.

- Joshua did forty days of recon in Canaan.

- Israel wandered the wilderness for forty years.

- A criminal got forty lashes max.

- For forty days, Goliath taunted Israel.

- The kings of the united monarchy—Saul, David and Solomon—all reigned forty years.

- For forty days, Satan tempted Jesus.

- For forty days, Jesus appeared after his resurrection.

- Women are pregnant for forty weeks.

- The army demands you do forty pushups.

Okay, those last two aren't specifically biblical, but you get the idea. There's a whole world of forties out there. What's with that? Is it sheer coincidence or some sort of Bible code? Well, it's not so much a code as a condition.

It seems God deems forty to be the appropriate period for testing, judging or proving something. Just about anybody can drop and give you twenty. But make it to forty, and we learn something about you. So, when it comes to testing, "Let there be forty."

Forty days of rain proves how dirty life on earth is. Forty years in the wilderness certifies the failure of an older generation, while creating faith in a newer one. Goliath's forty-day taunt confirms the cowardice of one king, while Satan's forty-day gauntlet proves the character of another. And if you can't get with the fact that the latter king ascended into heaven after forty days, well, his kingdom marches on without you.

Forty. It's God's favorite challenge.

As the conventional wisdom goes, when you're in your thirties, you're trying to prove something to others. But in your forties, you're trying to prove something to yourself. Perhaps during the transition you're doing both. And maybe God is in the audience.

The Dangers of Midlife

> *Nel mezzo del cammin di nostra vita,*
> *mi ritrovai per una selva oscura,*
> *ché la diritta via era smarrita.*

DANTE ALIGHIERI

Dante was about forty-three years old when he began writing the *Divine Comedy*, nearing the nadir of midlife. The year was 1308, centuries before we invented psychology. No matter. This translation of the above is perfectly apt for today:

Midway this way of life we're bound upon
I woke to find myself in a dark wood
Where the right road was wholly lost and gone.[1]

I (Greg) think the disorientation of midlife is hardwired into the human experience every bit as much as puberty. The times may change, but *this* time doesn't. Everybody goes through midlife. And in the dark wood, dangers abound.

We can fall off a cliff through our own blind wandering—like the strong man Samson who, somewhere in the middle of his life, started taking liberties with his holiness vow. As one called to be a *nazir*, meaning "separated" or "consecrated," this ancient knight was not permitted to consume alcohol, touch a dead body or cut his hair. But he brazenly did the first two, then foolishly permitted the third. Both the Lord and his strength left him (Judges 16:20), and Samson didn't even notice until it was too late.

We can fall prey to ravenous predators. As 1 Peter 5:8 warns, "Your enemy the devil prowls around like a roaring lion looking for someone to devour." And Peter knew what he was talking about. In the darkest moment of his spiritual journey, Satan nearly drained the faith right out of him, as three times he denied Christ.

We can fall into the hands of the living God. For reasons only he knows, God sometimes allows us to enter into a rigorous "forty test" when we least expect it. Deuteronomy 8:2 reminds us that Israel's forty years in the wilderness were designed to humble and test them, in order to reveal what was in their hearts. Similarly, somewhere in the middle of King Hezekiah's reign, circa 700 BC, God temporarily "left him to test him and to know everything that was in his heart" (2 Chronicles 32:31). And don't forget Job. His was the crisis to end all crises—losing health, wealth and family in a moment. When Job awoke, the wood was darker than any of us could fathom. But if he could hold onto faith and sanity, perhaps we can too.

(Mid)life

Midlife is a time unlike any other. It's a moment when we are able to look back at the first forty years of our life and gain a new perspective for the next forty, what we're calling 40/40 vision.

In our twenties, we're just starting out, feeling like lightweights. We wonder, *Can I hack it? Will I make it in the world? Will I do something significant? Be somebody who matters?* It's a decade of exploration and discovery, of testing the waters to find out who we are and what we're going to do. We want to figure out how we can make our mark on the world.

Our thirties are typically when we begin to experiment with

success. *How far can I go? How big can I make it?* This is not just about careers. Many of us start families and strive for success on that front too. It's a time of expansion as we move beyond our nomadic twenties into a more settled routine.

In our forties, the questions of life take a different shape. The achievements and successes seem less satisfying and no longer produce the same buzz. Whether you've achieved your dreams or not, you may lose a little drive. You may think about buying new pills or new wheels to enhance your drive. And with the first signs of waning strength, the really deep questions begin to surface. *All this work, does it even matter? I've striven for so long, but I'm still not there—and now I'm losing interest. Why am I not happier? Is this my lot in life? Did I miss my calling? Is it too late for a do-over? Was all that I pursued in my thirties a mistake?*

By age forty, we also begin to understand how quickly life passes. Just twenty years past, we were in college; just twenty years future, we'll be senior citizens. It's an inflection point, and often a tempestuous one.

Recently midlife surpassed the teenage years for the highest rate of suicide. Among middle-aged women, it's rising particularly fast. In 2011, the Substance Abuse and Mental Health Services Administration reported a 49 percent increase from 2005 to 2009 in drug-related suicide attempts for women fifty and older.[2] This disturbing trend is new, and it has something to do with the corrosiveness of the forties.

Lest you think this statistic a female anomaly, recent research shows that by age fifty women are *more likely* than men to report "a turbulent midlife transition" by just a couple percentage points (36.1 percent of women, compared with 34 percent of men), according to Elaine Wethington of Cornell University.[3]

Women tend to hit their most challenging midlife moments because of family turmoil like a parent's death, a divorce, an affair or disappointments in parenting. The tumult men face is more likely to result from work or career challenges.

In any case, midlife antagonizes us.

The Other Side of the U-Curve

But it's not all grim. Remember the U-curve of happiness and how midlife typically marks our lowest point? For many people, increased purpose and satisfaction lie on the other side—so for the joy ahead of you, endure the wandering into a new phase of life. And don't miss the satisfying points on the way.

A *New York Times* article identifying the benefits of midlife noted, "From many points of view, midlife permits us to be on top of the world, in control of our lives and well pleased enough with what we have accomplished to seek new outlets of both self-expression and giving back to society some of what we have earned—and learned."[4]

Nevertheless, midlife marks an important transition that most of us don't have time to navigate reflectively. Who has time to really think things through? With growing careers and families, there is more on our plates. More responsibility to carry, more bills to pay, more activities to attend. Our kids are growing, our parents are aging, and we find ourselves caught caring for two generations. Work-life balance is nonexistent. The marriage, family, house and body all need maintenance, but things fall apart faster than we can make repairs. "I just need another two hours a day," we sigh as we head to bed with the to-do list undone.

But stretched thin or not, the test of our forties demands our full engagement. We will emerge from this decade either proven or broken, either buoyed by hope or sunk by despair.

The outcome will not be determined by your past. Thus far you may have amassed smashing successes—or smashed dreams. You may be enjoying fruitful relationship—or ruing those that died on the vine. As we say, it is what it is. Honestly embrace the journey to date and consider how God has used your circumstances to shape your character. Then lean into the future.

We believe midlife outcomes hinge on the clarity with which you ask and answer the big questions of life. Questions like, *What is the meaning and measure of my life? What really counts? What future do I envision, and how do I get there?*

Psalm 90:10 reminds us,

> Our days may come to seventy years,
>   or eighty, if our strength endures.

Barring an early death, if you're in midlife there are still decades in your future. So let's get this pivotal decade right.

A Persistent Question

Questions of meaning are intimately human and personal. Whether you're a fourteenth-century writer or a twenty-first-century waiter, no amount of denial or distraction can silence them forever. Sooner or later they will be reckoned with.

Still, for many it's easier to put our heads down and keep plodding. Or to turn up the music and drown out the nagging voice. Or to focus on new hobbies and hope they will somehow bring fulfillment. Or to get a prescription to soothe our aching minds. But as a friend recently said, "In my thirties I pushed issues aside and just kept my nose to the grindstone. But now I'm finding that 'just keep working' isn't the right strategy anymore."

At age forty, German psychologist Erik Erikson developed a theory that psychosocial development has eight stages, and each stage provides an opportunity to develop a specific virtue. He postulated that in midlife we encounter a crisis of generativity versus stagnation where we face the question, *What am I here for?* The answer is basically a binary choice: me or others. Those who choose generativity selflessly invest in others and develop the virtue of "care."[5] Otherwise, they suffer stagnation, become self-absorbed and find that their lives lack meaning.

The rub, of course, comes from our impulse to selfishness. After twenty or twenty-five years of working hard and taking care of others, we want to join the crescendo of voices in our culture asserting, "I have to take care of me!" like Ray Kinsella talking to Shoeless Joe Jackson in *Field of Dreams:*

Ray Kinsella: "I did it all. I listened to the voices. I did what they told me and not once did I ask what's in it for me!"

Shoeless Joe: "What are you saying, Ray?"

Ray Kinsella: "I'm saying, [pause] what's in it for me?"

Embracing the Challenge

Before my (Greg's) son went to high school, I laid out a series of challenges to test his skills and fortitude—everything from cooking and cleaning to chopping down a tree and changing a tire. In one test I blindfolded him, drove him around town and then dropped him off on a random street. I said, "See you at home," then drove off.

Coaches, bosses and fiendish fathers sometimes do this sort of thing with their charges. We want to test them and know what's in their hearts. Don't worry: we live in a safe community; it was the middle of the afternoon; and my son had a cell phone (although there was a penalty for using it). In the end, he managed to wander home, and it didn't even take forty years—just three hours. But I was happy to hear that he passed one landmark three times before finally finding his way.

Frustrating challenges help us learn skills, solve problems and gain confidence. Afterward, we often say they were fun. Having finished my forties, I'm not quite ready to pronounce them fun, but they were informative and refining. Some moments still stand as the most challenging of my life. But I'm deeper and stronger in my fifties because of them. I might not be perfectly "generative," to use Erikson's term, but I do care.

The trick is not getting knocked out by the combination punch that forty hits you with. On the one hand, you're taking stock of the first generation of your life, and that can deal a real blow to the ego. Maybe you've lost a marriage, failed in a career or two, or gotten sidelined by an addiction or illness. Maybe you've had a child go off the ranch. Your story may not be an utter tragedy, but it's certainly not how you would have scripted it.

At the same time, you may be seeing dim prospects ahead. You top out at middle management, cap out in what you expect to earn. Your body begins to show some wear and tear. (I have a lengthening wrinkle on my left cheek that refuses to quit. It may be halfway down my torso by sixty.) And your life dream does that thing the sun does when it hits the horizon: fades fast.

That's when the midlife left hook threatens to turn out your lights. Like a weary fighter, all you can do is grab and hold.

The Wilderness

The flirtation at work. The gambling spree. The fantasy escape. With pain behind and ugliness ahead, your mind and body scream for something visceral and immediate: "We want to have fun, and we want it *now!*" But how quickly minor indulgences can became major lapses.

That's the bewildering side of forty. Things you once considered unthinkable become powerfully appealing. If nothing else, anticipate it.

If there's one place associated with forty more than any other, it's the wilderness. The place between Egypt and the Promised Land. The detour between Jesus' baptism and ministry. In the Bible, *forty* and *wilderness* go hand in hand. Thankfully, it's the place of difficulty we pass through, not the land we settle in.

In the wilderness, we experience austerity and ambiguity, what anthropologists call liminality. This rarely used word, derived from the Latin for *threshold,* describes our experience of the in-between. We're neither here nor there; we're caught in the middle. When a person goes through an ordeal or rite of passage, he or she feels liminal—disoriented and uncertain.

Think puberty. Does anyone feel secure and at home there? Not even close. Your body shoves you out the door of childhood, but you won't enter adulthood for years. You're stuck in between. You become a frightened, transitional life form. If you aren't careful, you may get eaten by seventh grade.

Midlife is like that. It's a second adolescence, composed pretty much of the same fears, questions and insecurities as the first one. In midlife, we experience liminality.

A friend of mine (Greg's) recently returned from a vacation in the wilderness of the southwestern United States. As an expert explained before he left, some cacti are actually edible. "But make no mistake about it," he added, "almost everything out there is designed to kill you." Which might prompt one to ask why a person would vacation there.

But as my friend insists, the wilderness offers both austerity and beauty. Just like midlife. The wilderness is a test: What will the result be? A or B? Austerity or beauty. Will we become severe and inwardly focused, or more noble and strong?

We are not the first ones to wonder. Or wander.

In exploring midlife, we benefit from guides. One, the writer of Ecclesiastes, has been described as an ancient writer with modern depression.[6] On the surface, that's not necessarily the guru you'd choose. But he asks the same questions we do about meaning and purpose, giving free rein to his darkest thoughts. And when life gets blurry, few things bring clarity like ancient wisdom.

MEANING(LESS)

How Do We Find Meaning
When Life Seems Pointless?

Everything is meaningless.

ECCLESIASTES 1:2

When I (Peter) travel, my airplane seat becomes a mobile desk and a haven of productivity. After quickly greeting my neighbor, I pop in my earbuds—effectively closing the door to my "office"—and get to work. I rely on this time to attack my inbox, write and prepare for the month ahead.

On a recent flight to Ukraine, I sat next to a very tall man with a Northern European accent, which I soon learned was Dutch. He began talking before I could place my earbuds. After pleasant introductions and some chatter about our travel destination, he asked the inevitable question: "So, what do you do?"

After describing microfinance, I began to describe how HOPE is a Christian organization seeking to address both physical and spiritual poverty. Clearly done with small talk, his eyes flashed as he firmly said, "I used to be a Christian, but then my son got sick. I begged God to save him every single day and offered God anything he wanted if he would just intervene and heal my boy. But there was no miracle. Watching my boy suffer and then die was the most gut-wrenching experience of my life. No parent should have to bury their child."

As I listened to more details of this father's anguish, my heart ached. He eventually concluded, "That was the last time I ever prayed."

Perhaps others wiser than I would have had a response, but hearing his excruciating story left my tongue tied.

After a few more minutes of conversation and then silence, I followed his lead and opened up the US Airways travel magazine from the seat pocket in front of me. Just inside the cover, a smiling pair of perfectly retouched swimsuit models stared back at me. A few pages later, I saw a ranking of the best plastic surgeons in America, three of which worked within driving distance of my home. An advertisement promised to freeze my love handles away. A little further on I found the cure for male pattern baldness. Then came a multipage spread detailing "5 Tips for Modern Dating," with an adjacent ad promising lonely travelers hope if we'll just dive into their pool of 200,000 potential matches. It's comforting to know they're as committed as I am to finding a soulmate.

In the wake of talking about death, this all seemed absurdly trivial. Seriously, what's the point of all that self-improvement when it so inevitably ends?

It wasn't just the pain of the man sitting next to me. By midlife, pain, death and loss have impacted us all. Grandparents are gone, and parents are showing signs of aging. We know we're not far behind as maturing takes its toll on our own bodies and minds. Our dreams begin graying as much as our hair. Life feels shorter than ever. The entertainments that used to keep us happy and distracted no longer produce the same thrill.

By midlife, our rose-colored glasses are cracked and foggy. Are we brave enough to take them off and squint into reality?

The Fault in Our Stories

The fault, dear Brutus, is not in our stars, but in ourselves.

WILLIAM SHAKESPEARE, *JULIUS CAESAR*

In John Green's wildly popular novel *The Fault in Our Stars*, we enter the story of two teenagers who meet at a cancer support group and fall in love against the backdrop of impending death.

Through the main characters, Hazel and Gus, Green explores places most young minds don't go. His characters ponder, *Who am I? What am I building here? And what will be left when I'm gone?* The sheer courage of their asking and the raw honesty of their answers is compellingly rare. (And when the author wraps that within a smart, well-written love story: gold mine.)

In Green's novel, cancer forces the characters to wrestle with deep questions early in life. For most of us, these issues don't arise until much later, after we've collected some lesser pains and disappointments. But sometime in our forties we ask, *Why is life so short, so hard, so pointless?*

Is there a fault in our stars?

No, but there is a fault in our stories. Most people believe life should be filled with rich experiences—not punctuated by them, but permeated with them. Each day should offer some new pleasure: a rewarding success at work, a fun adventure on vacation, a poignant moment at home. Some of us create social media avatars to portray our lives just this way. Look! A new taste, a new thrill, a new toy! Our online selves are as happy as clams. Meanwhile, our real-life selves are as *dead* as clams. (By the way, who picked the clam as a symbol of contentment?)

Like Hazel, Gus and my European seatmate, most people's reality is not an unbroken chain of beautiful moments and belly laughs. It's a hard slog. A shuffle through the ordinary and mundane.

A clumsy lurch through pain. Life is not without its pleasures, mind you, but the pleasures are the spice, not the main dish.

What if we were to face into that?

This Lightweight Life

The words of the Teacher, son of David, king in Jerusalem:
"Meaningless! Meaningless!"
says the Teacher.
"Utterly meaningless!
Everything is meaningless."

What do people gain from all their labors
at which they toil under the sun?

ECCLESIASTES 1:1-3

Fittingly, in the middle of the Old Testament is an ancient book of wisdom that is essential reading for the middle years of life. Though it was written more than two millennia ago, it reads like an angst-riddled movie script.

The protagonist is no Bible hero, no paragon of virtue and self-sacrifice. He's an antihero. A man living life on his own terms, pursuing one passion after another, only to come up empty. Reflecting on his experiences, he shares his hard-won wisdom, generally pointing readers in the opposite direction from the one he's traveled. He basically says, "I've been down that road, and it leads nowhere you want to go." He's offering us a chance to see *today* what we would otherwise realize only at the end. If we heed him, there's a good chance we'll find a more satisfying path.

The psychologist and Holocaust survivor Viktor Frankl advised, "Live as if you were living a second time and as though you had acted wrongly the first time."[1] That's the perspective of Ecclesiastes. We are invited to learn from another's midlife crisis, enabling us to avert our own, to journey through someone else's meaninglessness and find our own true purpose.

But before diving into the content, we have to understand the context. First, the title. *Ecclesiastes* obviously isn't a word we normally use. Occasionally we may hear a news story about an "ecclesiastical battle" of some sort. Or maybe you're a Bible student who knows the word *ekklēsia,* the Greek term that we typically translate as *church.* So why would this Old Testament book have a New Testament title?

Ekklēsia is a Greek substitute for *Qoheleth,* the Hebrew name of the book and its author. Qoheleth comes from *qahal,* an assembly or gathering, which is the literal meaning of *ekklēsia* in Greek. So when the Hebrew Old Testament was translated into Greek, they translated Qoheleth ("gatherer") as *Ecclesiastes.*

Now, if you're gathering people, it's for a reason. In wisdom literature, that reason is to instruct. So the gatherer is a teacher. Thus the proper name, *Qoheleth,* is often rendered *Teacher* in our English translations.

There's strong evidence that our teacher, Qoheleth, is supposed to be identified as King Solomon. Our first hint is his introduction as the "son of David, king in Jerusalem." Solomon was David's direct son and next in line for the throne. Later, we read that this person grew and "increased in wisdom more than anyone who has ruled over Jerusalem before" (Ecclesiastes 1:16).

If you know the story of King Solomon, you remember that as a youth he asked God for wisdom to govern the people well. Because Solomon made such an honorable request and didn't ask for riches, long life or the death of his enemies, God blessed him with all of the above. His wealth and wisdom were renowned, making Solomon both the wisest and richest man of his day—some say of all history. So as the mysterious Qoheleth tells his story, themed throughout with wealth, work, wine and women, it's not hard to discern who he is. If the author isn't literally Solomon, it's someone writing as if he were.

His tales of empire and glory hint not only at who wrote Ecclesiastes, but when. It's clearly a late-in-life memoir. He had finished his public works, amassed tremendous wealth and assembled a bevy of beautiful women. He had seen and done it all.

Popular wisdom has it that if Solomon wrote Song of Songs, it was probably in the spring of life, when he was flush with first love. He likely wrote Proverbs in the middle of his life, at the height of his intellectual and political power. And finally he wrote Ecclesiastes late in life, when the only thing left to tally was the true bottom line. Considering all of Solomon's accomplishments, from one perspective, his life is quite impressive. But it lacks one teeny, tiny thing: meaning. For Solomon, somehow it all feels absurdly worthless.

Ecclesiastes levels a withering attack on the presumptions of human ambition. Qoheleth soberly assesses all the chasing and toiling we do, deflating its value and deleting its meaning. Then he says, "There you have it: that's life."

Ecclesiastes is basically a crazed experiment in staring at the sun and describing how badly it hurts. *Life. What's the point? Where's the happiness and satisfaction? Does any of it mean anything?* But it's not nihilism. It's not the assertion that nothingness is everything. Qoheleth simply knows that you have to face the meaninglessness of your self-made life before you can find meaning from another source.

So he writes from a perspective *under the sun*—under the glaring light and relentless heat of our earthly grind. He invites his readers to forget, for the sake of argument, what life looks like with an intimate relationship with God. Instead, concentrate on this life—*just this life*—as if that's all there is. In other words, view it the way most people do. And then imagine another perspective.

To keep this thought experiment front and center, the Teacher repeats the phrase "under the sun" twenty-nine times. To be even clearer that he's envisaging life apart from *God*, he uses the word *Elohim*, a somewhat distant and impersonal title for God. This stands in contrast to *Yahweh*, God's relational, covenantal name.

So, with God out of the picture, Qoheleth describes the nothingness he sees. And that's precisely where we find the great worth of the book. Solomon spent his time and energy pursuing his own passions, leaving no desire unfulfilled, no stone unturned in a quest for meaning. His conclusion: "Take it from an old head like me before yours goes completely gray; most of what you think matters doesn't."

He understands the dangers of youthful and even middle-aged enthusiasm. He longs to impart some life-saving, course-changing wisdom. So he writes the epitaph for his own life: "Meaningless . . . meaningless . . . meaningless." That packs a sobering punch for all us strivers in midlife, especially as we consider his and others' accomplishments.

What's the Point?

At the end of his life, the greatest theologian of the Middle Ages, Thomas Aquinas, said, "I can no longer write, for God has given me such glorious knowledge that all contained in my works are straw— barely fit to absorb the holy wonders that fall in a stable."[2]

In the middle of his career, the great artist Renoir said he had reached the end of Impressionism and realized that "I knew neither how to paint nor how to draw."[3]

Leonardo Da Vinci summed up his brilliant career with, "I have offended God and mankind because my work did not reach the quality it should have."[4]

Meaningless, meaningless, utterly meaningless.

At some point we too will evaluate our life's work. We may strive and fail, wondering, *What's the point?* Or we may strive and succeed, wondering, *What's the point?* Or we may not do much striving at all and yet at the end—you guessed it—wonder, *What's the point?*

If the author of the *Summa Theologica*, a genius of Impressionism and the painter of the *Mona Lisa* said that about their work, well, pass the Prozac because I don't even want to think about mine.

Snapping at the Air

A few years ago, my (Greg's) family got a little black Labrador retriever for Christmas. We named him Blitzen, although *Blitzkrieg* would have been more apt, especially in the morning when we let him out of his kennel. That dog's energies knew no bounds. At any given moment, he just flipped out. (That's why my daughter called him Spazzy McGee.)

One day, I was sitting in the middle of the living room floor, reading. There was sun streaming through the windows, and Blitzen was sleeping soundly at my feet. Then, all of a sudden, he perked up. His head snapped to attention, his ears shot up, and he started snapping at the air.

I thought, *This dog is brain damaged.*

What could he possibly be doing? I puzzled for quite a while until I finally saw it. There were little specks of dust floating lazily in the sunshine, and Blitzen was trying to eat them. He wanted to catch them all, eat them and fill his stomach, but he kept coming up empty. Not that he missed. His jaws definitely clamped down on some dust. He just had nothing to show for his efforts. They were meaningless.

Meaningless is how some translators render the Hebrew word *havel*. "*Havel havalim, hakkol havel*," said Qoheleth. Utterly meaningless, everything is meaningless. The original Hebrew is lyrical and rhythmic. It's breathy, like sighing. Like panting. Like laughing. It's snorting at the cosmic joke that is this life. *Ha, ha, ha, ha.*

Havel is sometimes translated as *vain*, *useless*, *futile* or *absurd*. The root of the word means "vapor." It's something lightweight and ephemeral. It's insubstantial, and it's gone in a second. Solomon looks at life and calls it *havel*, a vapor, a breath. Eugene Peterson translates it as *smoke*. Another writer crassly paraphrases with *flatulence*.[5]

Many of us, like my puppy, wag and snap at a million things we want. We try to find substance in the trinkets big and small that money can buy. But the fuller our houses get, the emptier our souls feel. The more we acquire, the more we require. The sixth iPhone just doesn't do it for us like the first one did.

Maybe you're a sports fan. I (Greg) have a long and sad history of getting emotionally invested in my teams. Yet having spent nearly all my life in Philadelphia and Chicago, I've seen disproportionately few championships. One lousy Super Bowl. Two World Series. Michael Jordan was good to me, but most others have been disappointments. But here's the thing: even when "we" won, I was extra happy for about a day. Long seasons of caring netted mere hours of happiness. Qoheleth would call that *havel*.

When we see clearly, we realize that much of what impacts our emotional state just doesn't matter.

Scrutinizing the Earth

Now, to merely deconstruct human pleasures and pursuits is easy and unhelpful. Any fool can do it. But Qoheleth is a brilliant and creative freethinker whose book we classify as *Wisdom Literature*. As secular and godless as the text can seem, it helps us probe our fallenness. We get to grapple with our absurdities, confront our vanities, challenge our trivialities. The writer dissects and displays life, that we might study and learn.

And if he is really Solomon in disguise, we're talking about the most renowned sage in history. In 1 Kings 3:12, God tells him, "There will never have been anyone like you, nor will there ever be." Solomon was a man of unparalleled insight. He also happened to be fabulously wealthy and enormously powerful. He had the freedom and resources to explore all the tingles pleasure could bring, all the happiness money could buy.

So if the richest, wisest man in the world says it's all meaningless, it's worth considering his argument before we spend our lives in similar pursuits. And that's why God put Ecclesiastes in our Bibles. It guides us to the heart of nothingness, that we might seek life elsewhere. From that standpoint, Ecclesiastes is paradoxically devoid of gospel, yet full of grace.

The Parameters of Meaninglessness

Thankfully it's not entirely bleak. Qoheleth's opening assertion, "Everything is meaningless," is sweeping but not quite as absolute as it seems. He's just putting his thesis out there.

Like a great teacher, he follows it with a question:

> What do people gain from all their labors
> at which they toil under the sun? (Ecclesiastes 1:3)

There are a couple of terms here that establish the parameters of *havel*. The word *gain* is a business term. You work hard, and you expect some return on your labor. It's why you do what you do. You want to look back on your efforts and say, "I got from here to there, and I can count the profit." So comes a simple question: What advantage is to be gained from all our labors under the sun?

And the blunt answer: *None, if we are toiling for things that don't ultimately matter.* If your sole purpose in work is profit in this world, it'll all go to *havel* on you.

James Altucher, founder of Reset Inc. and StockPickr, said of his wealth, "I thought, if I could make 10 million dollars, then it must be too easy. In fact, I honestly thought everyone else had probably already made 11 million dollars. So then I felt poor again. I now needed 100 million dollars to be happy."[6] No amount of wealth, success or pleasure will truly fulfill us. At one point, Qoheleth says that God has placed eternity in our hearts, a universe-sized expanse that would swallow the whole world if it could—and still be hungry.

Next consider the word *sun* and our position under it. This is the writer's way of putting time and space borders on his angst. Qoheleth is writing from the perspective of this earth, under that blazing ball of gas—and that's the realm of the meaninglessness. It's about this time and place, this fallen world order. Qoheleth is essentially saying, "Where I live, right here and now, I can't find any lasting significance or meaning. For all my toil under the sun, I can't see even the slightest profit."

Qoheleth's analysis of life and his depressing conclusions are based on his choice to write from the perspective of life "under the sun"—a life with a distant, detached Creator. It's the perspective of a functional deist: a person who acknowledges God's existence but suffers due to his apparent absence. Because God is removed from daily life, the deist is left to find his own meaning. And without divine love or an afterlife, it's unattainable.

Today, few Christians would say, "I'm a functional deist," but the statistics suggest otherwise. A 2013 Harris Poll found that 74 percent of adults in the United States, the vast majority of us, believe in God.[7] But it's difficult to discern what difference that makes. Most theists have the same rates of depression and maladjustment as the rest of the population.

But we long for more.

T. S. Eliot wrote that we innately know we were made "for a further union, a deeper communion."[8] Or to use the oft-quoted line of C. S. Lewis, "If I find in myself desires which nothing in this world can satisfy, the only logical explanation is that I was made for another world."[9]

This is good news for midlifers, because we often dream of a life different from the one we find ourselves living. The eternity within suggests that while this world's *havel* might be as large as earth and as long as its history, there are other times, places and sacred spaces. Just because there is no meaning under the sun doesn't mean there is no meaning beyond it.

But let's not get ahead of ourselves. To bypass the hard realities would cheapen the final vista. Most of the learning is in the journeying. If you're going to Machu Picchu, don't take the bus; hike the Inca Trail. And if you're journeying from *havel* to heaven, well, there is no bus. You have to walk through the wilderness. Qoheleth has already traversed it, so he's well qualified to guide the way.

Another Perspective

On a dreary December day, I (Peter) was at the Philadelphia airport, ready for takeoff. Putting in my earbuds, I was reminded of the conversation with my Dutch seatmate a few weeks earlier.

I felt extra empathy for his pain, because those few weeks had been rough for me. In rapid succession, I had attended the funeral of a talented intern, dealt with corrupt government officials who offered no justice to those in poverty, and faced significant challenges with my children, which created stress in my marriage.

Life was hard, and God was not acting in ways that made any sense to me.

As the flight departed, we broke through the clouds, and the sun shone brightly. The bleak midwinter was replaced by majesty above. We weren't above the sun, but we were at least above the clouds. Below was rain and pain, but above was light and clarity.

Looking at all of life from an "above the sun" perspective is the only way to hope. This is the truth behind the truth of Ecclesiastes: life under the sun is not all there is. There is a different reality above the pelting rain and gloomy clouds.

Traveling in December, I was comforted that this is the month we celebrate the in-breaking of the Supernatural. As a newborn baby, God came to us. We don't have to ascend to him. He's here under the sun too.

(DIS)APPOINTMENT

How Do We Make a Go
When Life Doesn't Go As Planned?

Expectation is the root of all heartache.

UNKNOWN

W hen the very first flakes fell from the sky, my (Peter's) kids raced to put on their hats and gloves. They weren't the only ones delighted by the snow. It was December, and we were thrilled by the prospect of a white Christmas.

With just a dusting on the ground, we grabbed our sleds and headed to a nearby hill. Afterward, we returned home to steaming mugs of hot chocolate with extra marshmallows. In the background, Harry Connick Jr. exhorted us to be of good cheer. "It's the most wonderful time of the year," he sang. And it was.

By February, not so much. We lived in a world of slushy streets, toppled snowmen and dirty drifts. It was the most horrible time of the year. The evil queen Jadis made it always winter, never Christmas. Or worse: always home, never school.

More than fifteen school days were canceled. Parents seemed perpetually stuck at home with their kids. The first snow day is fantastic. The fifteenth is nearly fatal. Talk about the law of diminishing returns.

During life BC (Before Children), we had visions of happy little offspring and domestic bliss. When children finally arrived, life changed. Not that we weren't compensated with plenty of joy, but young kids can make a person feel rather constricted. We yearned to get a few years AD (After Delivery) under our belts.

But life being what it is, as kids grow up, we sometimes long to be *back* in the early years. When kids are small, the problems tend to be small. As they grow, the issues increase in size with them. I (Greg) recently heard a story of just how turbulent the high school years can be. Taking honors classes and making the varsity volleyball team, Amber began her sophomore year on a high note. But one day, the school nurse called explaining that Amber was sick. After arriving in the family minivan, Mom immediately saw the red circles around Amber's eyes and knew she had been crying.

"I slept with David," she sputtered, "and he secretly recorded it." And he was showing it at school.

Over the next weeks, life came to a full stop. There were meetings with the superintendent and guidance counselor. Lawyers were involved. As the proceedings continued, Amber switched to a private school. But the wounds were deep, both for Amber and for her family. "I was a failure as a mom and on public display," her mom said.

We expect to get out what we put in. That's the way it's supposed to work. You work hard, your career grows. You live wisely, you stay healthy. You parent well, your children thrive. Rationally we know it's not a foolproof formula, but emotionally that's what we expect.

But life "under the sun" is full of disappointments.

Not According to Plan

In moments of midlife honesty, we confess disillusionment with how life turned out. It might be with our kids or spouse, with our career or health, but the crisis happens in the gap between the ideal and the real.

Early on, we picture career fulfillment; after working a while, we feel career imprisonment. Before marriage, we imagine the bliss of having someone to complete us; after, we see our spouse as someone who impedes us. Before children, we want to coddle babies; later we want to cudgel teens.

No matter what your station in life, it can feel like the opposite would be better. Singles long for marriage while marrieds long for the freedom of singleness. Childless couples want kids while veteran parents look forward to the empty nest. Poorer people want more money, while richer people consider trading down to a forty-hour workweek and a modest paycheck. We long for a snow day—and just as quickly long for a return to school.

Long periods of disappointment can make escapist thoughts compelling. You're filled with visions of a life that looks different from the one you're living. Unchecked, disappointment can drive you crazy—and make you do crazy things. Todd Hendricks, a business leader, said, "*Woe is me* opens up a lot of bad doors." Keeping close company with discouragement is dangerous.

When I (Greg) was in my thirties, and even my early forties, I thought anyone who had a midlife crisis was a loser. *Grow up. You've got a great life, so why would you jeopardize it by doing something stupid?* That's the level of empathy I had for my angsty friends.

And then midlife hit me. With almost no warning, certain choices that were previously unthinkable began to feel plausible. Temptations that never attracted me before suddenly pressed in. My head was a jungle. I was disgruntled with my real life and captivated by a hypothetical better one.

For me, it was like standing on the bridge over the Royal Gorge or stepping onto the glass floor of the CN Tower in Toronto. I'm not a big fan of heights. When I visit these places, I don't typically linger long. I take a brief look into the abyss—long enough to prove my manhood—and then back away.

That's the way I had handled life-threatening temptations too: a brief glance and then a proper retreat to safety. But in midlife, I just stood at the edge and stared. I wasn't going to plunge to ruin—the bridge has railings; the floor is thick—but neither did I back away. I just stood there, entranced by the possibilities. What would it be like to do *that*? What if I went *there*?

It was a frustrating (and in retrospect, fascinating) place to be. There was the real possibility of forbidden thrills coupled with the conviction that you're just not going there. You might be disappointed, but you're not going to jump.

The actor Jim Carrey once mused on Twitter, "I think everybody should get rich and famous and do everything they ever dreamed of so they can see it's not the answer."[1] I'd stop short of recommending you actually do everything you dream, but Carrey has a point.

How do we handle the immense disappointments of life and the equally enormous temptations to take a flying leap into the new and unknown? I would start with a good long look, not into the abyss, but into the actuals of your life. Forty-seven times in Ecclesiastes, the Teacher instructs us to look. To examine. To press into the actual facts of this fleeting life.

Opportunity Costs

> *"Look," says the Teacher, "this is what I have discovered: . . .*
> *This only have I found:*
> *God created mankind upright,*
> *but they have gone in search of many schemes."*

Ecclesiastes 7:27, 29

In Pixar's 2009 film *Up*, we meet Ellie and Carl, a pair of childhood sweethearts who dream of exploring far-away places just like their hero, Charles Muntz. As kids, they make a pact that someday they will go to the top of Paradise Falls in South America. The two eventually get married and begin saving for their grand adventure.

Everything is going swimmingly until life happens. Flat tires, broken legs, new roofs. The coins saved for the grand trek are spent on pressing needs. Finally, in their golden years, the adventure is finally within reach. But in a devastating turn of events, Ellie dies, and the dream dies with her.

Pixar told this story in four minutes of visual poetry without a single spoken word. And if you don't cry openly as you watch it, you almost certainly choke back tears. Many list it among the saddest movie moments ever. As John Greenleaf Whittier wrote, "Of all the sad words of tongue or pen, the saddest are these, 'It might have been.'"[2]

It's a familiar script that hits close to home. By midlife, we've had opportunities that passed and will never come again. We've made mistakes that left permanent marks. A recent comedy features a slacker youth with "No Ragrets" tattooed across his chest. "That's my credo," he says proudly. "You have no regrets?" the dad asks. "Like not even a single letter?"[3]

The truth is that regret—no matter how you spell it—is our common language.

A nurse who worked in palliative care wrote an article revealing the regrets of her patients, confessed in the last days of their lives.

"I wish I'd had the courage to live a life true to myself, not the life others expected of me." . . .

"I wish I didn't work so hard." . . .

"I wish I'd had the courage to express my feelings." . . .

"I wish I had stayed in touch with my friends." . . .

"I wish I had let myself be happier."[4]

What strikes us is that each sentiment expresses an opportunity well within the person's reach. No one said, "I wish I had gone to Paradise Falls, but I never had the money." A bucket-list trip is a nice-to-have, not a have-to-have. No one's temporal happiness or eternal bliss rests on it. But personal integrity and human connection—these are the consequential things that yield either fulfillment or regret.

Qoheleth observed that God made us upright. God intended us to be full of integrity and capable of finding satisfaction through intimate, "upright" relationships with him and others. There's no need to chase schemes for overhyped happiness. The most worthy opportunities are free, but the opportunity cost of missing them is steep.

Say No to Nostalgia

> *Do not say, "Why were the old days better than these?"*
> *For it is not wise to ask such questions.*

ECCLESIASTES 7:10

People of a certain age begin telling stories about the good old days. Days when everyone worked hard and played fair. Days when kids played outside and rode bikes without concern for safety. Days when you could buy a tank of gas for what now fetches a bottle of soda.

The way our grandparents talk, you'd think everything was perfect back in the day. Morals were sky-high; crime was near zero. "All the women were strong, all the men were good-looking and all the children were above average."[5]

But people forget all the ways that the former days stank. Life expectancy was such that people often died right when they'd now be hitting their stride. Most families lost at least one child in infancy. Diseases went unchecked. Psychological problems went undiagnosed. And although you went outside to play, you also went outside to relieve yourself. Even in winter.

The word *nostalgia* tells an interesting story. It's a Greek word combining "return home" and "ache." It was coined by a seventeenth-century medical student to describe an unhealthy melancholy. Nostalgia can still be a medical condition—a constant backward look that not only puts an ache in your heart but a crick in your neck.

If you need a curative dose of reality, look no further than the Bible. Frankly, the Old Testament reads like an extended episode of *TMZ*, only with more violence and death. If you're looking for a cheery refrain like "Everything Is Awesome," you'll be supremely disappointed. Even the role models murder and commit adultery, and you can count the above-average kids on one hand.

In midlife, it's time to stop replaying the old tapes, or at least to stop letting them control you. Learn the lessons from your past, and then bravely move on. Stop looking back at what might have been. It's time to say no to unhealthy nostalgia. Better to point your gaze where it more naturally goes: forward.

A Handful of Satisfaction

> *Better one handful with tranquility*
> *than two handfuls with toil*
> *and chasing after the wind.*

ECCLESIASTES 4:6

Qoheleth's solution to midlife disappointment and restlessness is contentment. He says it's better to be content with what you have than to pursue what's *havel*. Later writers like the apostle Paul affirm the same truth. "Godliness with contentment is great gain. For we brought nothing into the world, and we can take nothing out of it. But if we have food and clothing, we will be content with that" (1 Timothy 6:6-8).

In the slums outside Mumbai, I (Peter) met Laila. The walls and roof of her home were made of corrugated tin. Walking in, I ducked my head to enter a small, dark room. The stale, suffocating air hung hot and thick. I took maybe six steps across the uneven dirt floors to cross the entirety of her house. My American eyes widened as I realized this claustrophobic room was home to a family of five. Laila invited me to sit on her one piece of furniture: a single bed that doubled as a sofa.

As I talked to the family, Laila's demeanor struck me. She didn't appear embarrassed at all. In fact, she rather proudly told me where she *used* to live. She was animated and gracious, and her spirit was lovely. In her cramped quarters, she was not only content, she was happy.

Obviously Laila's attitude was not a function of her circumstances. It stemmed from a deep surrender to the lot God had given her. She accepted her life for what it was, instead of bitterly wishing for what it wasn't. And rather than fixating on her troubles, she fixed her eyes on Jesus. In a situation that we would find impossibly difficult, she experienced strength, joy and peace. The Savior of the world was meeting her deepest needs, and it was clear that her hope was in him.

As I travel around the world, I find the gladness of people like Laila disturbing and challenging. How is it that some people in poverty find such joy and meaning in circumstances that would break us, who have so much?

By way of contrast, I (Greg) asked my colleagues the other day about Mindy, a star volunteer I hadn't seen in a long time. "Oh, she's no longer a Christian," I was told. "She's renounced it all. God didn't give her a husband, so she no longer wants to be with him."

Author Mark Buchanan noted, "One of the persistent cultural myths is the myth of fulfillment, the promise that on this earth, the fullness of all I truly need and all I really desire awaits. And it's not a Hollywood myth. It's a Christian one too. Maybe it's especially Christian."[6]

So many people think that God owes them a good life. They won't articulate it that way, but their expectation is that a modicum of obedience will yield a windfall of blessings. We did our good deeds; why didn't God reward us? We put our coins in the machine; why won't it vend?

If we could see more clearly, we'd discover that obedience does yield blessing, but not always in the form or time we prefer. The early Christians lived their good lives before God—and were imprisoned and killed as a result. "We must go through many hardships to enter the kingdom of God," they concluded (Acts 14:22).

Accepting the mystery of God, Qoheleth writes,

As you do not know the path of the wind,
    or how the body is formed in a mother's womb,
so you cannot understand the work of God,
    the Maker of all things. (Ecclesiastes 11:5)

Down with Expectation!

In order to be prepared to hope in what does not deceive,
we must first lose hope in everything that deceives.

Georges Bernanos

The disappointments in the middle of life can be a gift if they detach us from unrealistic expectations for this life. This isn't heaven. This life is not the be all and end all. Not that we despair of life, as if it held no joy or fulfillment. We just don't ask too much of it, and we seek to distinguish the truly meaningful from the briefly satisfying.

This world always commingles good and bad, pleasure and pain. Sometimes the mix is sweet, sometimes bitter. But God knows what he's about.

Jesus said, "Which one of you, if your son asks for bread, will give him a stone? Or if he asks for a fish, will give him a snake? If you, then, though you are evil, know how to give good gifts to your children, how much more will your Father in heaven give good gifts to those who ask him!" (Matthew 7:9-11). Believing this reframes everything.

Having difficulty parenting? You were chosen by your Creator to raise this child. The good gift you might expect is not a perfectly good kid, but a good measure of physical endurance for the early years and emotional strength for the later ones.

Struggling at work? Your vocational calling is every bit as valid as the pope's and the president's. At the same time, your calling is so much larger than your day job. Ask God for insight into whether you should stay put or move on. And ask him to round out your vocational contribution with other good works that satisfy.

Facing a health issue? You were assigned this circumstance by your Creator, to live faithfully in the midst of it. When the apostle Paul couldn't get rid of his thorn in the flesh (whatever it was) he received a promise: "My grace is sufficient for you, for my power is made perfect in weakness" (2 Corinthians 12:9). I've never met a Christian who doesn't think that promise also applies to the rest of us. On the medical front, you must decide how aggressively to seek healing; and on the spiritual side, seek power for *dealing* too.

Expect problems. Also expect power.

Shakespeare supposedly once said, "Expectation is the root of all heartache." (Was he a Buddhist? I hadn't heard.) But Paul had at least one expectation that was the root of all hope: the power of Christ. He knew life would throw him plenty of fastballs up and in. But he discovered the secret of contentment, whether his circumstances were good or bad: he could do everything through Christ, who strengthened him (Philippians 4:12-13).

People of faith actually "do all things"—some of them extremely difficult—in this mode. An African nun who works with AIDS orphans in the slums of Nairobi does it. She describes her daily life this way:

> We rise very early and say our prayers together, after which we eat a small breakfast. Then we awaken the children, dress and feed them. After our mid-morning prayers, we return to care for the children. We eat a very light lunch, say our prayers together and take a short rest; then we return yet again to serve the children. In the late afternoon we gather for prayer, which is followed by supper. After feeding the children and putting them to bed, we pray one last time and then retire for the evening. This is my life![7]

Sounds to me like snow days on endless repeat. What drudgery. I couldn't do it. But when Jerry Sittser (who you'll learn more about later) heard this account, he said that what struck him was the woman's tone of voice and facial expression. She seemed utterly at peace—serene and content.

Somehow she had grown to accept her calling and find fulfillment in the mundane. Could we do that? What if one of the developmental tasks of midlife is to work through our discontentment?

Up with Appreciation!

The great British preacher Charles Spurgeon once said, "Curb your desire and you have struck at the root of half your sorrow."[8] That's a true Christian perspective. Desiring a situation you can't create yields despair, so curb your desire. But Spurgeon says that only solves half your sorrow. What about the rest of it?

Try gratitude, the twin virtue of contentment.

Ann Voskamp, the author of *One Thousand Gifts*, challenges people to list three things each day for which they're grateful. These could be big or small things, from a healthy child to a piece of chocolate. But you have to list them *in writing* each day. That will cost you.

You'll have to find a pen. And paper. And thirty seconds of time.

Here's what you can expect in return:

- A relative absence of stress and depression
- An added ability to make progress toward important personal goals
- Higher levels of determination and energy
- A closer feeling to others and a desire to build stronger relationships
- 25 percent more happiness[9]

This is backed by science, which Ann cites. One expert in the field is Sonja Lyubomirsky, a professor of psychology. She writes, "The more a person is inclined to gratitude, the less likely he or she is to be depressed, anxious, lonely, envious, or neurotic."[10]

Gratitude, intentionally expressed three or more times a day, is a pretty low-cost way to get high-octane results. In the words of Jesus, "Now that you know these things, you will be blessed if you do them" (John 13:17).

Divine Appointments

Here's the reality: there are times in life when we simply do not understand the ways of God. It's a mystery why tragedy occurs to some and not others, and why God leaves dreams unfulfilled. But it's nothing new. As Qoheleth said, "Then I saw all that God had done. No one can comprehend what goes on under the sun. Despite all their efforts to search it out, no one can discover its meaning. Even if the wise claim they know, they cannot really comprehend it" (Ecclesiastes 8:17).

But disappointments can become divine appointments with God. When life under the sun discourages us, we can look beyond the sun, adjust our vision and invite new dreams.

For Kellie Haddock, life certainly didn't turn out like she planned.

Fourteen weeks after her first child was born, Kellie and her husband, along with baby Eli, were in a horrific car accident. Her husband died instantly, and Eli was in critical condition. If he survived, Eli was not expected to be able to walk, talk or show emotion. "My world fell apart in an instant," Kellie said. "From all being as it should be to suddenly finding everything in a million pieces around me. I felt like I was left standing there in the middle of the rubble and I didn't know which way was north."

After a night of intensive prayer, Eli began showing signs of improvement. It became clear that he would live, though there was no way to tell how much his injuries would affect his development.

In an instant, Kellie had gone from newborn bliss to being a widow and single mom of a child with special needs. Disappointment, to say the least. Yet she experienced a sweetness and intimacy with God in those days that defies circumstance.

Five years after the accident, Kellie remarried, and her second husband, Ted, adopted Eli. Glowing with fiery red hair, Eli can walk, talk and show plenty of emotion, despite the doctors' initial predictions.

In a radical display of others-centered gratitude, Kellie decided to celebrate the ten-year anniversary of the accident by finding the doctors who saved Eli's life. She visited each one of them and invited them to an event in their honor. Many of the doctors said they'd never before been thanked for their service.

"This whole journey has been such a mix of the darkness right next to the beauty," Kellie said. "We are ten years and counting into our journey of healing and though at times it's been harder to see, God's sufficiency has never wavered."[11]

As the Teacher observed, "He has made everything beautiful in its time" (Ecclesiastes 3:11).

(IN)SATIABLE

What Happens When the Thrill Is Gone?

There are two sources of unhappiness in life.
One is not getting what you want; the other is getting it.

GEORGE BERNARD SHAW

I n 2014, immediately after winning Super Bowl XLVIII, Malcolm Smith, the game's MVP, was in his glory. As the confetti rained, the Seattle Seahawks star was asked, "What are you going to do next?" His response: "I'm going to Disney World!"[1]

This catchphrase, a brilliant marketing strategy, has been uttered countless times since Phil Simms first said it after the New York Giants' Super Bowl win in 1987. We've heard it from the likes of Magic Johnson, Tony Dungy, Dwyane Wade, Tom Brady, Eli Manning and Pedro Martinez. We've heard it from non-athletes like David Cook, Kris Allen, Lee DeWyze and Scotty Mc-Creery, who all said the Magic Kingdom words after winning *American Idol*.

Disneyland—no, Disney *World*—promises happiness levels beyond all others. In fact, it was Walt Disney himself who proclaimed

it "the happiest place on earth." Super Bowl wins? Recording con-
tracts? *Please.*

I (Peter) waited until I was thirty-nine to visit the Magic Kingdom
for the first time. Lili, my eight-year-old daughter, accompanied me.
We both were excited—Lili to meet the cast and characters, and me
to create a lifelong memory with my daughter.

We started our visit with a tour of a small museum housing original
artwork from the Disney archives. We also saw the original bench
from Griffith Park in Los Angeles, which had sat near the old merry-
go-round where the idea of Disneyland was born. Walt Disney remembered the day:

> Well, [the idea for Disneyland] came about when my daughters
> were very young and Saturday was always Daddy's day with the
> two daughters. I'd take them to the merry-go-round and as I'd
> sit there, sat on a bench, you know, eating peanuts, I felt that
> there should be some kind of an amusement enterprise built
> where the parents and the children could have fun together. So
> that's how Disneyland started.[2]

That's a great vision, almost like heaven. A carefree haven where
everyone has fun. A place to fulfill the universal longing for a
kingdom of happiness.[3]

Walking through an archway, Lili and I saw a large picture of
Sleeping Beauty, with the words "From this slumber she shall wake
when true love's kiss the spell shall break." We experienced the Toy
Story ride and remembered that even old toys found a new home
when Andy went to college. Many of us want to believe it's true that
there's a happily ever after for each of us. So we make the pilgrimage
to one coast or other, just for a foretaste. But we quickly realize that
the happiest place on Earth isn't always happy.

I heard a child begging for cotton candy—while licking an ice-
cream cone. I saw a woman frantically patting her hair after getting

off Space Mountain, apparently concerned that she was looking alien. I saw dads transfixed by the phones in their hands, oblivious to the children at their feet; families in tight spaces agitated by the long lines; employees biting their tongues when dealing with cranky customers.

Just another day in paradise.

You don't need to be a theologian to realize that if Disneyland is the happiest place on earth, it's only an indictment of the planet. Personally I've never heard anyone say, "You know what? It's exactly what the slogan says!" We walked away with tired legs, expensive souvenirs and no reason not to set our hopes on heaven. (But if you've never been, by all means make the trip. Everyone should have to go at least once.)

Pleasure-Soaked Emptiness

We live in a world saturated with pleasures. Good pleasures. God-built creature comforts everywhere. Green grass, blues skies and warm sunshine. A hard run, a good joke and the smell of frying bacon. Clean sheets. Hearing Mozart in a concert hall, U2 in a stadium and a daughter's delight at Disney World. There's something good and right about all of it. Simple, sensory, satisfying pleasures.

But here's the paradox: pleasure is both ever-present and ever-fleeting. It seems like the very moment you have it in your grip, it's slipping through your fingers. When you're young and naive, you assume the longer-lasting kicks come later. *When I get married, then I'll be content. When I get that promotion, then I'll be fulfilled. When I've been there and done that, then I'll truly be gratified.*

But few things can satisfy, and nothing can satiate. And the really diabolical twist is that the older we get, the kicks aren't longer; they're shorter. That's why Bono still hasn't found what he's looking for, Mick Jagger still can't get no satisfaction, and pastors and authors still quote those two songs.

But that doesn't mean we won't try and try and try and try.

Testing Ourselves

*I said to myself, "Come now, I will test you with pleasure to find out
what is good." But that also proved to be meaningless. "Laughter," I
said, "is madness. And what does pleasure accomplish?" I tried
cheering myself with wine and embracing folly—my mind still guiding
me with wisdom. I wanted to see what was good for people to do
under the heavens during the few days of their lives.*

ECCLESIASTES 2:1-3

Who hasn't experimented with hedonism? We turn on Netflix to
watch one episode, then go to bed after ingesting an entire season.
We eat three bites, then inhale the whole bag. We pour one glass,
then polish off the bottle. (It wasn't full when I started, was it?)

And our pleasure centers just mock us. As Ravi Zacharias said,
"The loneliest moment in life is when you have just experienced what
you thought would deliver the ultimate—and it has let you down."[4]

It's fascinating to ponder Qoheleth's confession about testing
himself with pleasure. Note that he didn't test pleasure. He tested
himself using pleasure. Pleasure was just the Bunsen burner; its
heat tested his heart. And what a conflagration he lit:

I undertook great projects: I built houses for myself and planted
vineyards. I made gardens and parks and planted all kinds of fruit
trees in them. I made reservoirs to water groves of flourishing
trees. I bought male and female slaves and had other slaves who
were born in my house. I also owned more herds and flocks than
anyone in Jerusalem before me. I amassed silver and gold for
myself and the treasure of kings and provinces. I acquired male
and female singers, and a harem as well—the delights of a man's
heart. I became greater by far than anyone in Jerusalem before
me. In all this, my wisdom stayed with me. (Ecclesiastes 2:4-9)

Not only was the king wealthy and powerful, he also enjoyed the perks that came with the position. Marshaling his resources, Solomon ate and drank, planted and built, sang with his friends and slept with his harem. He pursued every pleasure previously advertised, then invented a few new ones of his own. His was the original Magic Kingdom, and he was the magician.

Of course, we know what he's going to pronounce it all: *havel.* Nothing.

That's helpful information for midlifers who think they said "I do" to the wrong mate and contemplate the bed of another. Or the person thinking about uprooting a stable family to chase a dream job in another state. Or the one considering a costly and time-consuming vacation home as the panacea for midlife drudgery. Qoheleth did everything you're pondering.

But it's still tempting. The pull of pleasure intensifies in midlife. And we want so badly at least to dabble in it. Like the old saying, "I know money can't buy happiness, but I'd still like to try."

Knowing we were writing this book, Ryan, a friend who leads a Christian ministry, shared his midlife pleasure test. It wasn't as large or lecherous as Solomon's, but just as dangerous and empty. He wrote:

> I have a story that's embarrassing to tell but might help some people. Proverbs says, "Guard your heart above all else, for it is the wellspring of life." In my midforties, I didn't do that, and it nearly consumed me.
>
> It started innocuously enough. I knew a woman who was just a little more special than my other female friends. Not that I rank women; I was just fond of her.
>
> So I paid her more attention. We interacted fairly regularly anyway, but I found myself enjoying her company more and more, so I extended conversations. I turned on the charm and tried to be funnier. I went out of my way to run into her. I had

no intentions of doing anything; I was just overworked and bored. This relationship was my balm—my little cloud, shading me as I was "under the sun."

To be honest, I occasionally had these crushes before. Even though I was happily married, every once in a while I felt an attraction. But I never did anything with it and always got over it quickly. But your forties can be like your teens, like a second adolescence. Whatever the reason, I wasn't getting over this one.

So in a very short time, three things happened. One, I had the opportunity to serve this woman and her family in a fairly significant way. Gift giving is my "love language," so this probably meant more to me than it did any of them. Two, I saw some photos of her and became very curious about her life. Three, I downloaded some old songs from high school and decided the love songs were about her.

All I can say is that it was like terrorists kicked open the door of my heart and hijacked my emotions to Cuba.

Overnight I went from puppy love to utter preoccupation. I couldn't *not* think about her. Days I knew I might see her were great days. Days I knew I wouldn't were pointless. Soon my "shade cloud" was following me like Eeyore. It was torture. I tried to pray about it and reason myself out of it, but my heart was having none of it. I couldn't shake it. I had ginned up these emotions that had nowhere to go.

When I net it all out, it was basically fun for two weeks and miserable for two years. It was the single biggest struggle of my life.[5]

This was just a midlife crush! Scary. Pleasure-testers beware: in midlife you might open a Pandora's box that you can't close again.

I (Peter) picked up the phone and called Ryan to thank him for his honesty, and we talked for quite a while. He said the real pain wasn't just his, but his wife's—because eventually it came out. His wife saw him pulling back at home, detached, sometimes surly, less interested in her and the kids. She knew something was wrong and pressed him to tell her. But he denied his struggle for months, leaving her stressed and unhappy.

Finally, a year after it began, Ryan came clean. Immediately he felt better, but of course his wife felt worse. That's when their relationship hit rock bottom. They had to slog through all their issues, doing the hard work of confessing, forgiving and reconnecting. It took time. Ryan said, "In the end, my wife suffered even more than I did. She hurt while I was going through my issue—and long after. To this day it still pains her at times, like the grief that suddenly rears up at the memory of an old loss."

That's another aspect of the cautionary tale: the impact of our lunacy isn't just ours to bear. Our lives are webbed together with our family and friends. When one person suffers, everyone does. If one person's emotions go AWOL, everyone else has to bear the burden.

Thankfully Solomon doesn't sugarcoat his exploits with, "Yeah, I made some mistakes, but what a ride! I wouldn't change a thing!" That's called folly. And arrogance. Solomon is both wiser and more honest:

> When I surveyed all that my hands had done
>> and what I had toiled to achieve,
>>> everything was meaningless [*havel*]. (Ecclesiastes 2:11)

Commenting on pleasure tests, the ancient rabbi Geniba told a story about a fox and a vineyard:

> A fox happens upon a beautiful vineyard, but he cannot enter. It is walled in on all sides. Then he discovers a very small hole, but it is too small to pass through. So, being a shrewd fox, he

fasts for three days and then, lean and weak, slips in.

He proceeds to feast on all the food before him. But when he tries to leave, again he cannot fit through the opening. So he fasts for three more days and then, lean and weak, wriggles his way home.

Turning to the vineyard, the fox says, "O vineyard, O vineyard, how good are you and your fruits inside! I can't say anything against the vineyard. It's good. All that is inside is beautiful and commendable. But what enjoyment has one from you? As one enters you, so he leaves."[6]

Post-Party Depression

The eye never has enough of seeing,
nor the ear its fill of hearing.

ECCLESIASTES 1:8

Everyone's toil is for their mouth,
yet their appetite is never satisfied.

ECCLESIASTES 6:7

At the end of Christmas day, my (Greg's) kids invariably say, "I'm bummed that Christmas is over." All the buildup is thrilling, but the pleasure passes before we've thrown away the wrapping paper. I feel those blues too.

But, hey, you can always eat your way back to happiness. I remember one December 26 a few years ago. I slept in, then had a late breakfast consisting of two items: ham and pecan pie. Lots of ham and two large slices of pie. I had my salty, I had my sweet, and it was excellent. But the rest of the day I kept chasing. I ate a box of Nerds—straight sugar—so naturally I followed it with some pretzels. But then

I missed that sweet sensation, so I found some chocolate. By the time that was gone, I needed more salt. *Hey, who took the cheese curls?*

I stayed on that bender through the New Year. I wish I could say it was *havel*, that the net gain was zero, but it wasn't. It was five. Thomas Merton once wrote,

> No one who simply eats or drinks when he feels like eating or drinking, or smokes whenever he feels the urge to light a ciga-rette, or gratifies his curiosity and sensuality whenever they are stimulated, can consider himself a free person. He has re-nounced his spiritual freedom and become the servant of bodily impulse. Therefore his mind and his will are not fully his own. They are under the power of his appetites and through the medium of his appetites, they are under control of those who gratify his appetites.[7]

That's a wordy way of saying that pleasure is a trap. You give yourself to pleasure, then you're "given over" to it. Thinking you're the master, you freely indulge. But next thing you know, you're a slave. As 2 Peter 2:19 reminds us, "People are slaves to whatever has mastered them."

Whether our appetite is for food, sex, money or some other thrill, we actually become hungrier when we indulge. We stretch our stomachs, creating even more space to fill.

MalFUNction

> *A person can do nothing better than to eat and drink and find sat-isfaction in their own toil. This too, I see, is from the hand of God, for without him, who can eat or find enjoyment?*
>
> ECCLESIASTES 2:24-25

Sports Illustrated told the story in 2010 of the University of Ala-bama's national football championship, dubbing it the beginning of the dynasty. Yet the article described Coach Nick Saban as "stern-looking" and his facial expression as a "semigrimace." The author went on to say that "those best equipped to win championships are often the least equipped to celebrate them."[8] But why? Why the imbalance between stimulus and response? Why so little pleasure? Why couldn't Saban smile?

Despite the emptiness of so much pleasure, Solomon asserts that there is much satisfaction to be derived through simple things like tongues, taste buds and daily toil. The problem is, our pleasure meters are broken. Under the sun, in our fallen condition, we have insatiable appetites but little capacity for enjoyment. Things just aren't as fun as they should be.

Years ago, ice skater Nancy Kerrigan, after winning an Olympic silver medal, was given the rare opportunity to tell the cameras of her intentions to go to Disney World. But a few weeks later, she made headlines when, sitting next to Mickey during her parade, she was heard muttering, "This is corny. This is so dumb."[9]

I thought Olympic skaters were practically born Disney princesses. I'd have no problem with a Stanley Cup winner calling it dumb and corny, but a figure skater? *There's a magical, glittery parade in your honor. You can't enjoy that?*

But now we're talking about us, not Nancy. The apostle Paul wrote that God "richly provides us with everything for our enjoyment" (1 Timothy 6:17). We're blessed in a billion ways. My goodness, we're *literate*. Right now you're *reading a book*! How many other people only wish they could? Yet in midlife, this and a myriad other pleasures don't register.

Thus confronted, most people just take a few moments to try to be happier. They count a few blessings. They chew slower. They stop and smell a rose. There's nothing wrong with that and much right about it. But reflect more deeply. This malfunctioning pleasure center of ours is a gift. It's a grace. If we were satiable apart from

God, would we ever seek him? If this present kingdom were magical, would we pin our hopes on the one to come?

It's good when the thrill is gone. We were made for another world.

Pleasure Plan

Many people are familiar with the first stanza of the Serenity Prayer— the bit about what can and cannot change and the wisdom to know the difference. But that's only the first stanza. The rest goes like this:

> Living one day at a time,
> enjoying one moment at a time,
> accepting hardships as the pathway to peace,
> taking, as He did, this sinful world
> as it is, not as I would have it,
> trusting that He will make all things right
> if I surrender to His Will,
> that I may be reasonably happy in this life
> and supremely happy with Him
> forever in the next.
> Amen.[10]

Those last lines right-size our expectations. Living under the sun, we can expect to be *reasonably happy* now. But connected to the God above the sun, we can expect to be *supremely happy* later. Surrender to God, enjoy his gifts and seek a higher goal beyond your personal happiness.

If you obsess over the question "Am I happy?" it's likely you never will be. But free yourself from the expectation, and you may be. C. S. Lewis said, "Aim at Heaven and you will get Earth 'thrown in': aim at Earth and you will get neither." It's another paradox: if you don't expect utter fulfillment from earthly pleasures, you'll be better equipped to enjoy them. Ecclesiastes 6:9 puts it this way:

Better what the eye sees
   than the roving of the appetite.

Here too is the gift of midlife. We experience food, sex, money, power, family and friends. They both satisfy and dissatisfy, but in this stage, our focus often falls on *dissatisfy*. So, what do we do next? Eat more food? Get a new family? Seek a bigger and better experience?

We in the modern world conceive of happiness as an experience-based phenomenon. That's partly why we claim inalienable rights to pursue it. We believe in life, liberty and the pursuit of happiness. But many people in the Majority World prove that neither *life* as we conceive it nor *liberty* as we know it are necessary for *happiness* as we crave it.

Happiness studies in the prosperous West bear this out too. Daniel Gilbert, one of the top researchers on the subject, studied the happiness of two groups of people: lottery winners and paraplegics. Surprisingly there was no difference between the happiness of the two groups. Yes, initially there is a rush of raw pleasure after winning a lottery and a deluge of despair after suffering an injury causing paraplegia. But after a few months, the vast majority of people in both groups were no happier or sadder than they were before. Well, except for the lottery winners; a significant portion of them ended up *less happy*.

Gilbert writes,

From field studies to laboratory studies, we see that winning or losing an election, gaining or losing a romantic partner, getting or not getting a promotion, passing or not passing a college test, on and on, have far less impact, less intensity and much less duration than people expect them to have. In fact, a recent study—this almost floors me—a recent study showing how major life traumas affect people suggests that if it happened over three months ago, with only a few exceptions, it has no impact whatsoever on your happiness.[11]

Other studies reveal the *havel* of so much so-called happiness, especially as it relates to money. The happiest US demographic earns $50,000 to $75,000 a year.[12] The Amish are as happy as billionaires. A friend makes you 15 percent happier,[13] while getting a $10,000 raise makes you only 2 percent happier.[14]

It's Not the Destination, It's the . . .

Journey. Most of us know this. The process means so much more than the product. Qoheleth writes,

> My heart took delight in all my labor,
> and this was the reward for all my toil. (Ecclesiastes 2:10)

It's not the destination; it's the getting there.

Kids love Legos. My (Greg's) son once got two pricey kits as gifts, the kind that cost three figures. We spent hours putting them together and had a great time doing it. But when the Legos are built, what do you have? An unwieldy Star Wars contraption that your son plays with for a fraction of the time he spent building it. The product is nice, but the real pleasure was in the process.

But what if you could marry the process and end product? Jackpot.

Two of my friends from church, Jack and Sarah Smith, had finally "arrived." They were living in the right home, in the right neighborhood, with the right jobs. They were out of debt, having paid off their mortgage, and were enjoying life with their two boys. About to enter midlife, they considered themselves blessed by God, but also deserving of the lifestyle they had created for themselves. After all, they had worked hard during the first half. Looking back, Jack says, "We were continually seeking to fulfill our own desires and just hoping to sprinkle a little bit of God on top, when and where it was convenient and practical."

But something significant started happening as they reengaged with church and started studying the Bible. First they were convinced they should give away all the money they had saved to redo their kitchen. Then they felt compelled to just sell the entire dream home.

Concerned family and friends wondered what they were doing. "Why would you leave behind your perfect house and make such a poor financial decision?" Had they gone on a midlife shopping spree, people would have applauded, but this radical generosity seemed ludicrous. Yet they were loving life as they were loving Jesus.

After reading David Platt's *Radical*, they decided to write a "blank check" to God and trust him to make a plan better than anything they could create. As they prayed, "Lord, what do you want me to do with _____ (our money, our house, our belongings)," they felt the Lord answer clearly. "If Jesus said go to all the world, we needed to go," Jack said.

So, eventually they moved to a Muslim country to share Christ with people who have little interaction with followers of Jesus. Jack and Sarah could be living it up, but instead they're living it *up*. Theirs is a God-ward life pointing beyond the sun.

Their life verse is Psalm 37:4:

Take delight in the LORD,
and he will give you the desires of your heart.

Jack reflects, "As we look back, it is interesting to see how our desires have become simply to follow Christ and live at his feet."

Satisfaction guaranteed.

Where the Party's At

Solomon pursued every pleasure on this horizontal plane and came up empty. But his father, David, went vertical. Despite his escapade with Bathsheba (darn you, midlife!), he did a U-turn and was known as a man after God's own heart. Knowing the emptiness of things under the sun, he sought pleasure in God and wound up full.

Describing the opposite of his son's *havel*-ish pursuits, David said,

> You make known to me the path of life;
>> you will fill me with joy in your presence;
>> with eternal pleasures at your right hand. (Psalm 16:11)

In other words, God is where the party's at.

The Westminster Catechism puts it this way: "Question: 'What is the chief end of man?' Answer: 'To glorify God and to enjoy him forever.'" John Piper puts a twist on it, saying, "The chief end of man is to glorify God *by enjoying him* forever."[15] And he calls this Christian hedonism.

So, in God's presence is fullness of joy. By delighting in him, we receive the desires of our heart. Apparently we humans are satiable creatures after all.

George Mueller was a nineteenth-century hero of the faith who worked with orphans in England. His autobiography is still in print, and in a chapter entitled "Walking in Darkness," he tells of an insight that came to him one day in his middle years:

> I saw more clearly than ever that the first great and primary business to which I ought to attend every day was, to have my soul happy in the Lord. The first thing to be concerned about was not, how much I might serve the Lord, how I might glorify the Lord; but how I might get my soul into a happy state and how my inner man may be nourished.[16]

"Get my soul into a happy state." How exactly would one do that? Mueller's advice starts with something that might sound horribly predictable: read your Bible. He writes, "The most important thing

I had to do was to give myself to the reading of the word of God and to meditation on it."[17]

But it's not just that you read, it's *how* you read. Don't just read for a little axiom to guide your day. Don't just read for a bromide to soothe your pain. Instead, read to see above the sun, to gain a grand vision of God.

John Piper says this: "No one goes to the Grand Canyon to increase their self-esteem."[18] He means the Grand Canyon is massive and spectacular, and you don't go there for anything but to be blown away by the vista. The same is true when surveying God in the pages of Scripture. You open a Bible to gaze at him. And when you truly see his attributes and actions, it's a pleasure beyond compare: "We are wired to be satisfied by admiring the most admirable, and the most admirable is God," Piper says.[19]

Simple Steps

Seeking pleasure in God can begin quite simply. Jeanne was coming out of an exhausting season of mothering when there was little time (zero, to be precise) for a personal agenda. Her plate was full keeping five kids alive. But last fall, when most of them were back in school, she found time and space to go out on a limb.

A Facebook friend posted an urgent need for volunteers to stay overnight at a local women's shelter. Jeanne felt a quiet nudge to sign up, which she did. But when the time came to get in the car with her sleeping bag and pillow, she wasn't looking forward to it. At all.

Upon arrival, her misgivings were confirmed. She felt completely out of place. "What does a country bumpkin with a cushy life have to offer street-smart women?"

But what a difference a night can make. Despite feeling awkward, Jeanne jumped in and started conversations with the women and found she clicked. There was a real connection, and it was as life-giving to her as it was to them. The next morning she drove home to her husband and exclaimed, "I am so tired, so terribly unqualified, and yet I have never felt more alive!" Jeanne experienced the pleasures of God. The color and passion returned to her life, and she knew she was living for something satisfying.

What a contrast to those who slink off at night for different reasons, only to return feeling dirty and diminished. When the thrill is gone, pursue it again in God and don't stop until you find it. He himself promises to be discovered by you. "You will seek me and find me when you seek me with all your heart" (Jeremiah 29:13). Only you can learn and know what it means to seek God with that kind of passion, but the payoff promises to be fantastic.

(IM)MORTAL

How Can You Find Clarity in a Casket?

Remembering you are going to die is the best way I know to
avoid the trap of thinking you have something to lose.

STEVE JOBS

On our anniversary a couple years ago, Laurel and I (Peter) stopped by Ephrata Community Hospital to visit my Grandpa Ellison. He'd spent his life serving as a pastor in Pennsylvania. Walking the white hospital hall, I was flooded with memories of him—how he'd taught us grandchildren the fine art of Ping-Pong; how his blue eyes twinkled just before serving his young opponents; how his prayers would point our family to our heavenly Father.

As I stood by his bed, something felt different. His breathing had changed. The color had drained from his sunken cheeks. And the hospital staff was acting especially tender toward us.

After a few minutes, a nurse took us aside and gently told us that they were going to take him off oxygen with my grandmother's consent. My grandfather had instructed that he not be put on a respirator.

In the presence of the ones he loved, this beloved man stepped out of this life and into the great beyond. My regal grandmother collapsed over the body of her childhood sweetheart and wept.

The following Saturday, our family gathered at the memorial service to share remembrances of a man loved and respected by so many. "Your grandpa was a special person," a gray-haired man commented as he shuffled through the receiving line. "One time, we were playing golf, and you know, we were never very good. We invited a group to play through, and by the time they passed us, he knew everything about them. Their names. Their kids' names. Where they worked and what they enjoyed. He knew how to care for people."

He continued. "And do you know how we met? Years ago I drank and smoked too much, and I thought he was too much of a goody-goody. So I went up to him and said, 'Hey, preacher, what's wrong with you? There's no big deal with drinking and smoking. I am free to do as I want.' And do you know his response?" Without waiting for me to guess, the man continued, "All he said was, 'That's true, but I am free to choose not to.' It wasn't judgmental, but it was powerful. Turns out, that was the start of a friendship unlike any I ever had."

Too often, you never fully know the impact of a person's life until they are gone. After my grandpa's death, I was told story after story about the ways he loved and served others. The stories extended far beyond the pulpit, where he had faithfully preached each Sunday to his small Philadelphia congregation.

After the memorial service, family members caravanned to the graveside, where we shared a few more brief words and prayers. "Ashes to ashes and dust to dust, unto the Lord's hands do we commit your soul," my father concluded. Then he encouraged everyone to say a final goodbye. One by one, folks sadly approached the grave before turning toward their cars and heading to the reception.

Not ready to leave, I watched the cemetery staff lower Grandpa's coffin into the ground. They kneeled on the fake green grass around the four-by-eight-foot chasm and loosened the straps that were balancing the coffin above the hole. As it was lowered, I could hear it clunking against the earthen walls. A backhoe was not far away to fill the hole.

I tried to wrap my mind around what I was being asked to do: say goodbye to my grandpa. There was no coping mechanism to fall back on, just raw grief to feel. But I saw with new clarity the brokenness that sin had wrought in the world. It was all right there in a wooden coffin.

God never intended death (except his Son's). Death was the result of sin and will end in eternity.

For our family, that Saturday afternoon altered the course of our lives. It changed every birthday party and holiday gathering, every dinner table where his absence was felt. The men burying Grandpa didn't known that the precious man they lowered into the ground was the keeper of a thousand family memories. They didn't know the delight he felt tossing his grandchildren into the air just to see them laugh or the way his eyes sparkled when telling a story. They didn't know the way he had cared for his wife since the day they said, "I do."

At the gravesite, my mother grabbed a shovel and began scooping dirt onto the grave. The cemetery staff stepped back, giving us space. More family members joined in. We shoveled in silence until all we could see was a pile of earth.

Clarity in a Casket

> *It is better to go to the house of mourning*
> *than to go to the house of feasting,*
> *for death is the destiny of everyone;*
> *the living should take this to heart.*

ECCLESIASTES 7:2

Life's most unpleasant certainty is this: we are going to die. No matter how hard we try to fight it or forget it, we all have an expiration date. Statistically, in our forties, we are closer to the tomb than the womb. Soon they'll cart us off the field. The game will resume, but we'll be gone. Yet we want to call a time-out and extend the game as long as possible.

Death is impossible to ignore during midlife. For many of us, grandparents pass, making us aware that our parents are next. Almost no one makes it through midlife without putting on a suit and walking through a cemetery. And many have prepaid with unspeakable grief earlier in life.

Qoheleth states that it is better to enter a house of mourning than a house of feasting, to weep in sorrow rather than laugh in joy. He values how death brings life into focus. Pastor Colin Smith writes, "Every person should attend a funeral at least once a year. Going to a wedding reminds you that the marriage bond is sacred. Going to a funeral reminds you that life is a vapor and one day yours will be gone."[1]

Almost everyone walks away from a funeral a bit more thankful for the life and loved ones they have. The most bereaved may not feel it, but the rest of us do. We feel a little more love, a little more gratitude, a little more urgency to make every day count. We realize that we have no dominion over death, but we do over our daily decisions. We can make better, more purposeful choices—and often at a funeral we determine to do so.

The question facing us is, "How can we lay this to heart?" We don't go to the house of mourning every day, so it's easy to slip back into our old ways. How do we incorporate both the reality of death and the felicity of life into the motivational center of our souls?

Fire and Fertilizer and Faith

In Greek mythology, at the dawn of human history, every person knew the day of their death. But when the Titan Prometheus had a falling out with Zeus, things changed. Prometheus was known for stealing fire from the gods, enabling humans to light the darkness, warm their bodies and forge new technologies. But he stole something even more consequential, and not from the gods but *from us.* He stole our knowledge of the day of our death. In its place we were given blind ambition, the illusion of control and the belief that we could live forever.

Originally this was a cautionary tale, reminding people not to think too highly of themselves or to believe themselves to be immortal. But over time, Prometheus became the champion of modern thinkers who believe that with our "fire" we can do just about anything we put our minds to.

A cover story in *The Atlantic* features an old man on a skateboard along with the title "The New Science of Old Age."[2] The contributing editor, Gregg Easterbrook, reports how experts are predicting that by 2084, life expectancy for Americans will be one hundred— *without* any great technological advances. We're just trending that way. But genetic science holds great promise for lengthening that term. After all, every single human cell contains the DNA code for replicating itself in a healthy new form; we just have to help those cells keep doing that.

Some of our greatest thinkers believe that with just a few more breakthroughs, we will live forever. Promethean ambition abounds. But in his Pulitzer-winning book *The Denial of Death*, anthropologist Ernest Becker attempts to knock some sense back into us.

> Creation is a nightmare spectacular taking place on a planet that has been soaked for hundreds of millions of years in the blood of all its creatures. The soberest conclusion that we could make about what has actually been taking place on the planet for about three billion years is that it is being turned into a vast pit of fertilizer. But the sun distracts our attention, always baking the blood dry, making things grow over it and

with its warmth giving the hope that comes with the organism's comfort and expansiveness.[3]

The world is a fertilizer factory. Not a happy prospect. In another passage, Becker suggests that to live honestly and to take life seriously, we must live aware of the "rumble of panic underneath everything."[4]

So the idealist says, "We'll beat death!" And the realist says, "There's nothing but death!" How about a third option?

The Day of Death Inspires Good

Samuel Johnson famously said, "When a man is to be hanged in a fortnight, it concentrates his mind wonderfully."[5] And many a near-death experience has affirmed his observation.

When Flight 1549 emergency landed on the frigid Hudson River in January of 2009, it could have been catastrophic. It *should* have been. But thanks to Captain Chesley Sullenberger, the crew and passengers experienced "The Miracle on the Hudson." Afterward, the passengers made statements like these: "There must be a reason." "There must be a meaning and purpose. I need to find out what it is." They promised to be better husbands and wives, mothers and fathers. And they began regularly gathering for "celebrate life" parties in Charlotte, North Carolina, where many of the passengers lived.

"Everyone on that flight feels they were given a second opportunity," said survivor Pam Seagle in an interview with *The Guardian* a year after the crash. "We struggle with the need to do something with it. Should I leave my job? Should I devote myself to charity? We must redeem our lives. We must make sure we don't waste the gift we've been given."[6] A kind of transformation comes when we realize that we aren't invincible, but we are purposeful. We're not immortal, but our lives have meaning. That's why Becker says, "Man cannot endure his own littleness unless he translates it into meaningfulness on the largest possible level."[7]

This is the invitation issued by midlife brushes with mortality. Not that we have to redeem our lives—only God can do that—but that we get to live intentionally, as those who have already been redeemed.

Nothing to Lose

> *Surely the fate of human beings is like that of the animals; the same fate awaits them both: As one dies, so dies the other. All have the same breath; humans have no advantage over animals. Everything is meaningless. All go to the same place; all come from dust, and to dust all return. Who knows if the human spirit rises upward and if the spirit of the animal goes down into the earth?*

ECCLESIASTES 3:19-21

The question is, What does it mean to live a redeemed life?

On many levels, Ecclesiastes is a brilliant experiment in missing the point. With God out of the picture, the brevity of life could easily be translated into a mandate to eat, drink and be merry, for tomorrow we die. After all, who knows if the human spirit lives forever? Who knows if it meets God, to whom it's accountable? The only sure thing is today. Thus pop singer Sia wails a pathos-laden

> I'm gonna swing from the chandelier, from the chandelier.
> I'm gonna live like tomorrow doesn't exist, like it doesn't exist.[8]

But suppression of the truth is a losing strategy. It turns death into a Voldemort—"he who must not be named"—for fear that the very mention of the word will make it more substantial and real. And so those diagnosed with cancer sometimes refuse to speak the C-word. And those suspecting Alzheimer's refuse to apply the scarlet A. Maybe that's not always wrong-headed; maybe it's a way of keeping your chin up or fighting the good fight. But often it is what Becker decried as not taking life seriously. In doing so, we deny death.

The truth is, a power shift occurs when we name death and its minions. And the power goes to the namer, not the named. There is no need to fear saying "cancer" or "Alzheimer's" or "death." When you say, "Midlife isn't working. I'm losing my bearings. I'm cresting the hill, and I'm afraid of the other side," you don't give it power. By naming it, you take a kind of dominion over it. You face the opponent head-on rather than shadowboxing an unnamed enemy. And you begin to acknowledge that victory in the fight does not mean beating death, but meeting it nobly.

Dr. Mario Garrett, a professor of gerontology, notes a deficit in end-of-life counseling, even among people of faith: "With the medicalization of death, there is a passive acceptance by faith leaders that death is a medical event rather than a spiritual journey."[9] And since death is a spiritual journey, people need guidance.

One such guide is a chaplain who works with people in hospitals as they face their own mortality. He has come across all types of folks: some who resign early and some who seem determined to deny death to their last breath. When all the therapies have failed and all the life-saving measures have fallen short, they hold on to a vain hope for a miracle.

When he works with those who insist on a miracle, he tactfully names the elephant in the room: "While we continue to pray and to believe in the God of miracles, who can do anything, it appears this disease is going to run its course. Can we talk about that?" A wave of relief often sweeps the room. The patient and those with him are usually liberated from excessive optimism. Someone has named death, enabling everyone to come to grips with it.

How does acknowledging death liberate people? First, the patient and family can begin to consider impending hardships honestly and make preparations. Second, they can better savor their remaining time together. Third, they are free to say how much they love each other and to address issues of conflict and make amends. People who persist in rejecting death don't get to say their last words to each other. They don't want to acknowledge death, and it overtakes them with business left on the table.

Living Gratitude

Kristine was living in Pennsylvania and wasn't able to attend her grandfather's funeral in Florida. Her close relationship with him made the sting of missing the event that much more painful. One Sunday, as she talked with a friend at church, she shared the news of her grandfather's passing. Despite having never met the man, the friend began to weep. With tears flowing down her cheeks, she entered into Kristine's pain. Her companionship and empathy allowed Kristine to mourn with her when she couldn't mourn with her family.

For Kristine, this compassion overflowed into concern for others struggling with pains and sorrows: an aunt who was struggling with drug and substance abuse; friends in the midst of a marital catastrophe; even her husband, who was watching his own grandfather's health decline.

All suffering is a function of death at some level.

The house of mourning makes the human condition, which often masquerades as comfortable and easy, painfully real. It spurs a deeper connection to those who hurt, which is central to a meaningful life. It made Kristine's future hope more precious, because she believes that the human spirit does rise, finding peace and rest beyond this life. And it makes Christ's spiritual presence more valuable, knowing that he didn't cling to his place in the house of feasting but instead entered the house of mourning to both experience death and remove its sting.

Live Your Eulogy

How would things be different if we lived every day in light of our deaths? In an attempt to explore this, I decided to write my eulogy.

When I (Peter) first told Laurel about it, she laughed and said I was crazy. When I told her I wanted to invite my family and friends to my fortieth birthday party and read it to them, she knew I'd lost it, and she said, "You really need to finish that midlife book and move on."

Perhaps unsurprisingly, my eulogy had nothing to do with the things on my résumé, nothing about my jobs or titles. It had everything to do with people, with issues of faith and love, and with gratitude to God and others. And I did read it at my party, where we ate carrot cake, because carrots make it healthy, right? And then we went on imperfectly loving each other.

That exercise allowed me to see the stark contrast between eulogy virtues and résumé virtues.[10] It's far too easy to spend our best energies building résumés and our last days regretting it. In the end, none of those accomplishments matter so much. And beyond our eulogy, when we stand before God, will the successes of even the biggest world-changer look anything but petty?

The most significant gift I received for my fortieth birthday just might have been the gift of considering my mortality—and living and loving just a little bit differently as a result.

A Life Well-Lived

John R. W. Stott died in 2011; he was ninety years old. The rector of All Souls Church in London, he preached thousands of sermons, wrote over fifty books and founded Langham Partnership International, an organization that aids pastors and missionaries. He did a thousand other noble things too.

And while his is quite an impressive résumé, it wasn't these feats that left the most indelible marks. Upon Stott's passing, Tyler Wigg-Stevenson, who served as his assistant, wrote, "It is John Stott the disciple of Christ that I mourn today, rather than John Stott the Evangelical statesman. For in my year with him, he continually revealed the Lord to whom he had given his life, whole cloth."[11] Right up to the end, Stott routinely invested in those younger than himself. Tyler was one of those privileged individuals.

Imagine the impact of a year alongside Stott, especially in his twilight. The man had come to a healthy acceptance of death years before his time was up. In 1973 he wrote:

> One of the most searching tests to apply to any religion concerns its attitude to death. And measured by this test, much so-called Christianity is found wanting in its black clothes, its mournful chants and its requiem masses. Of course dying can be very unpleasant and bereavement can bring bitter sorrow. But death itself has been overthrown and "blessed are the dead who die in the Lord" (Revelations 14:13). The proper epitaph to write for a Christian believer is not a dismal and uncertain petition, "R.I.P." (*requiescat in pace*, "may he rest in peace"), but a joyful and certain affirmation "C.A.D." ("Christ abolished death").[12]

It was with this confidence that, on July 27, 2011, three of Stott's oldest friends stood at his bedside, reading 2 Timothy aloud while Handel's *Messiah* played in the background. As the chorus sang, "I know that my Redeemer liveth," Stott passed, his final spiritual journey complete.[13]

Stott's passing illustrates the steps to dying that have always been part of classic Christianity. Rob Moll lists them: "Expressing willingness to die, showing belief in Jesus, offering final thoughts and encouragements to family and friends, giving hope in the life to come—[these] do more than create a peaceful and welcoming environment for the dying person. These actions prepare the spirit."[14]

And they don't only prepare the spirit of the dying, but also the spirits of those who live. Basic to Christianity is a willingness to die, to take up your cross daily and follow Jesus. Paul said, "I face death every day" (1 Corinthians 15:31).

Perhaps nowhere else is the contrast between over- and under-the-sun perspectives more pronounced. Under the sun we see garbage. We see caskets. We see fertilizer pits. But with God above, we see grace. We see victory. We see death evaporating into a new dimension of life. Jesus said, "I am going there to prepare a place for you" (John 14:2). Therefore, we can say with confidence,

Where, O death, is your victory?
Where, O death, is your sting? (1 Corinthians 15:55)

(UN)CHARITABLE

How Do We Build True Wealth?

If a person gets his attitude toward money straight,
it will help straighten out almost every other area in his life.

BILLY GRAHAM

As we got ready for a date night after a packed week, Laurel and I (Peter) were primed. We had our babysitter lined up and our restaurant picked out. And the promise of chicken masala already had our mouths watering.

As Laurel got ready, I grabbed the day's stack of mail and began opening envelopes. The mortgage payment greeted me, followed by the heating bill, the water bill and the credit card bill for a piece of plastic I didn't even know we had.

When Laurel walked downstairs, I decided this would be an excellent time to talk about money. After fifteen years of marriage, you would think I'd know better. I'm sure somewhere among the seven billion people on this planet, there's one who considers checking account balances an aphrodisiac. But, darn the luck, I'm not married to her. So we spent a rather chilly evening together.

Truth is, most couples would rather read a dictionary than talk about finances. Few topics are more contentious, and in fact, Kansas State University researcher Sonya Britt found that arguing about money is the top predictor of divorce.[1] No other factor even comes close. But we avoid the topic and blindly hope that financial problems will fix themselves. Meanwhile, the stack of bills keeps growing, leaving the average American hemorrhaging cash.

Many of us feel financial pressure most acutely around midlife, as paying for our children's college and preparing for retirement loom large. Exacerbating the pain, we recall years of youthful carelessness and kick ourselves for not being more frugal. We've worked for twenty years and have less to show for it than we hoped.

For some, the pressure isn't about feeling unprepared for the future; it's about drowning in debt. Consumer debt is a stumbling block to satisfaction in midlife. Right when we'd like to take advantage of all the vacation time we've accrued, the bank balance vetoes our plans. Worse still, all that debt prevents many from living out the vision and purpose God has for them.

Ironically we are living in the wealthiest period in human history, yet most of us feel less than rich. And for the select few who have achieved financial independence, the money doesn't deliver the bliss they expected.

The March 2011 *TIME* magazine cover story focused on "10 Ideas That Are Changing Your Life." Idea number seven, "High-Status Stress," began like this: "What if the good life isn't really all that good? What if the very things so many of us strive for—a high-paying, powerful job; a beautiful house; a wardrobe of nice clothes in desirably small sizes; and a fancy education for our children to prep them for carrying on this way of life—turn out to be more trouble than they're worth?"[2]

The article continued by showing how all the benefits we thought we'd get from wealth actually disappear. "Once you get affluent enough, the mental and physical health benefits associated with greater affluence fade away. In fact research indicates that as you near the top, life stress increases so dramatically that its toxic effects essentially cancel out many positive aspects of succeeding."

As Qoheleth says,

> The sleep of a laborer is sweet,
>   whether they eat little or much,
> but as for the rich, their abundance
>   permits them no sleep. (Ecclesiastes 5:12)

Stress and money are like conjoined twins. We can't separate them, so we have to take them together.

A Little Bit More

> *Whoever loves money never has enough;*
> *whoever loves wealth is never satisfied with their income.*
> *This too is meaningless.*
>
> ECCLESIASTES 5:10

The Bible speaks of money in over 2,400 verses. It's a subject mentioned three times more than love and eight times more than prayer.[3] It's a topic of particular interest to wealthy sages like Qoheleth, who wrote from the perspective of the world's wealthiest king, when his country was an economic superpower. For Solomon, all of his drinking vessels were of pure gold, he "became greater than all the kings of the earth in riches and in wisdom," and he "made silver as common as stones in Jerusalem" (1 Kings 10:21-27 NASB).

As his reputation grew, the Queen of Sheba came to visit and exclaimed, "The report I heard in my own country about your achievements and your wisdom is true. But I did not believe these things until I came and saw with my own eyes. Indeed, not even half was told me; in wisdom and wealth you have far exceeded the report I heard" (1 Kings 10:6-7). Yet despite his record-setting accumulations, near the end of his life, Solomon came to the same conclusion as so many others: it's never enough.

It's amazing to read his words and recognize that, nearly three thousand years later, we're feeling the exact same thing. We might not be drinking our grog from golden mugs, but Americans have accumulated a shocking amount of stuff. Our houses are bigger than ever before;[4] we have more cars than we do licensed drivers;[5] and in an effort to pay for it all, we work thirty days more each year than our grandparents did.[6] We have so much stuff that the storage business is one of our fastest-growing industries.[7] Advertisers tell us how to get it, and reality shows tell us how to get rid of it.

Our formula for living looks something like this: Stuff + More Stuff + Even More Stuff = Extraordinary Happiness. If that were true, Americans would be the happiest people on earth. But we aren't. We're not even in the top ten, according to the World Happiness Report 2013.[8] We are, however, the world leader in antidepressants, making up two-thirds of the global market.

In exploring the ancient issue of greed, Dennis Okholm writes, "We have strong desires for products before we have them, but once acquired, they mean very little to us."[9] He cites research showing how people focused on material wealth "are less content than others with their lot in life and tend to be more anxious, depressed, distressed, not as well adjusted, and experiencing lower levels of well-being."[10]

We accumulate lots of stuff that fills our basements but not our hearts. And no matter how much we have, there's never quite enough. When John D. Rockefeller, the first billionaire, was asked how much would be enough, he famously replied, "A little bit more."[11]

"Yeah," you say, "but I'm just a thousandaire. I actually need a little bit more."

Meet a hundredaire. The Democratic Republic of the Congo has been crushed under the weight of poverty. The annual per capita

GDP was only $484 in 2013,[12] and more than 70 percent of the population lives under the national poverty line.[13] Most will likely die by age fifty.[14]

Beleaguered by civil war, disease and blatant corruption, the DRC is the last place I expected to find contentment and generosity. Yet it's home to remarkable people like Kangudia. Her husband had been out of work since the Congolese civil war, so in a desperate attempt to make some money for her family, Kangudia set up a small bread stand on the side of the road. She didn't earn enough to feed her family of seven, so they made the gut-wrenching decision to eat just one meager meal every two days. Kangudia and her family were starving.

One day, Kangudia's ten-year-old daughter came to her with a knife in her hands, confessing that she wanted to take her own life. With tears in her eyes, she told her mother that she'd rather die quickly by stabbing than slowly by starvation. Kangudia was filled with despair and cried out to God to provide.

Not long after, a microloan of fifty-five dollars allowed Kangudia to expand her business, an opportunity that could potentially fill their bellies a little bit more. She began selling tea and coffee in addition to bread. Slowly her small stand became a sort of roadside Starbucks in the streets of Lubumbashi. Within a few months, she was feeding her family daily and sending all of her five children to school. She even became successful enough to double the size of her house, a far more important change in her situation than in ours.

While that sounds like the proverbial "happily ever after," her story doesn't end there. Unable to ignore the rampant poverty around her, Kangudia decided to spend God's provision on her community. From the Bible, she learned that God's people are supposed to care for the widows and orphans, and she didn't see an exemption clause. She simply assumed that God was speaking to her. Today,

Kangudia singlehandedly provides for her pastor and his family so that he can focus on full-time ministry. She also provides for a local widow and her family. On top of that, she gives 10 percent to her church. Kangudia lives a life of extravagant generosity and has a contagious and obvious joy in giving herself to others.

What amazes me (Peter) is that Kangudia is not giving begrudgingly or waiting until she gets all her financial ducks in a row. She's doing it now.

And she's not alone in this type of overflow. I'm aware of countless people across the world who live like she does—people who truly understand that it is more blessed to give than to receive.

And these generous people don't just live in exotic, developing-world locales; some of them live right in our backyard, in our cities and towns. The financially poor in the United States have a much better record in giving than their wealthy peers. There is actually a *negative* correlation between income and generosity in this country—that is, the more you make, the less you give. The poorest fifth of Americans give away 4.3 percent of their earnings, while the richest give away 2.1 percent. The most generous group in the United States is "the working poor," many of whom are recent immigrants.[15]

When times are tough financially, those with less income tend to continue giving steadily, while the richest Americans taper off. Paradoxically, while these modest-but-generous people own less, they have more—more happiness, more contentment and more fulfillment—than their stingier neighbors.

What is happening here? Is it possible for those with less to have a more meaningful experience under the sun? In my work in places of financial poverty, I have had my own spiritual and relational poverty exposed, while being humbled by the faith, hope and love of those with much less stuff. What is the secret to finding wealth beyond possessions?

We Enter and Exit Empty-Handed

Everyone comes naked from their mother's womb,
and as everyone comes, so they depart.
They take nothing from their toil
that they can carry in their hands.

This too is a grievous evil:

As everyone comes, so they depart,
and what do they gain,
since they toil for the wind?

ECCLESIASTES 5:15-16

There's a story about a wealthy man who was about to die from a terminal illness. He wanted to be buried with his cash, so he called three pastors into his hospital room. He gave each an envelope containing $100,000 and asked them to place the envelopes in his coffin before he was buried. "I know I can trust you," he said, perhaps with more hope than confidence. All three pastors agreed.

A short time later, the man died. Each pastor showed up at the funeral and placed an envelope into the casket before it was lowered into the ground. At the reception afterward, the three pastors gathered. One pastor asked sheepishly, "Did you leave the whole amount in the envelope?"

The first pastor responded, "Well, it's been a tough year, and our church needed some repairs. I didn't think he'd mind if I took $20,000 out and left the rest."

The second pastor was visibly relieved. "I did the same thing. We really needed a new bell choir, and we had a mission trip heading to Guatemala. So I took $30,000 and buried the remaining $70,000."

The first two turned to the third pastor and asked what he'd done with the money. "I put in the whole thing," the pastor replied. "But I wrote a check."

You can't take it with you—but others can and will take it from you. Here's how Al Hsu, author of *The Suburban Christian*, described the "accumulation curve":

> Imagine a bell curve. We start at zero and we end with zero. In between, we acquire a certain amount of stuff, so there's an upward slope at first. It makes sense in our twenties that we're getting stuff for our apartment or first home. But at some point we have enough and the curve should level off. Then in midlife and older, we start to get rid of stuff, because we don't need as much and can't take it with us anyway. So we practice generosity and give stuff away. Some people, like hoarders, never stop acquiring and never start giving. Their line just keeps going up until they die, and then their crammed-full houses end up on reality shows. Other people learn to live within their means and to say enough is enough, and their bell curve is flatter than most.[16]

Midlife invites us to consider what's in our wallet and what's in our heart, to consider what we will do with our wealth while it's still in our hands. Think of your bank account as the written account of your life's passion. More than anything else, money is a thermometer, taking the temperature of our hearts. In our forties, we do well to reset the thermostat until the thermometer reads what it should.

The Science of Giving

Biology has proven that when we give, we really do receive a high. The part of the brain that activates when receiving "rewarding stimuli"—the ventral striatum—fires when we give to others.[17] This is the same reaction that comes when we see a beautiful piece of art or go for a run. Call it a giver's high.

Other studies demonstrate the same results: we become happier when we give. Those who have the largest budgets for giving tend to be the most satisfied. One study showed that people are happier when they are shopping for others than when they are shopping for themselves. Participants were given a small sum of money, from five to twenty dollars, along with simple instructions. Half the group was free to spend the money either on themselves or on others, while the second group was instructed to spend only on themselves. Afterward, the people who spent money on others were significantly happier.[18] That's the blessedness that God built into his grace-and-generosity economy.

Appetite for Giving

In the United States, we've developed super-sized appetites for pleasure, but we haven't experienced a corresponding rise in our taste for giving. Robert Putnam's well-known research, reported in his *Bowling Alone*, identified an alarming downturn in charitable giving:

> Trends in American philanthropy relative to our resources are dismaying, for in the 1990s, Americans donated a smaller share of our personal income than at any time since the 1940s. . . . In 1960, we gave away about $1 for every $2 we spent on recreation; in 1997, we gave away less than 50¢ for every $2 we spent on recreation.[19]

Selfishness is trending—and has been for decades. But it's not just "other people" who are caught in the flow. As I (Peter) researched these issues and did a little self-examination, I found that the stats aren't about America but about *me*. When I looked back over my tax returns, I saw exactly the same trend. As my income increased, the percentage of my giving decreased. In fact, my percentage of giving was highest when I was living in Rwanda and earning $24,000 a year.

Recognizing a need to change, our family is working to follow the example of friends who committed to giving at least one percent more every year. This simple step is helping our family to acquire an appetite for generosity while also accruing true wealth.

Practice the Power of Giving

It shouldn't take another stock market crash to remind us that wealth accumulation is *havel*. But we're so hardwired to hoard that it's hard to change. And some of us have dug deep holes. We'd like to give, but we just can't see how we can afford it. Plus we have kids engaged in expensive activities that we're convinced are integral to their growth. Who wants to rob them to give to others?

If you've never developed generous habits before midlife, it's a very challenging time to change. But it can be done.

Recently my wife and I (Peter) had a much overdue conversation about finances. (Not on date night.) We pored over our expenditures, wondering where all the money had gone, and found that we hadn't made a single major purchase. It was all nickel-and-dime stuff: CVS, Walmart, Target, Dunkin' Donuts, Amazon. It was death by a thousand paper cuts. And really, what did we have to show for it?

If we wanted to become more generous, we had to become prudent on a daily basis.

One of the best habits I know is writing down everything you spend. Log it each day. In a week, you'll see how quickly the discretionary spending adds up, and it'll give you pause the next time you think about a frivolous purchase. Do that simultaneously with disciplined, automated giving to your church or other charity, and you'll find you can redirect a nice monthly sum—with virtually no pain. If you're hardcore and want to feel your sacrifice, then by all means cut deeper!

But it's easy to avoid giving. Just do what you've always done. No one will ever know. Greed is anonymous. Unless you run for political office, your record will never come to light—unless, of course, you believe in the day when *everyone* stands before God and *every record* comes to light.

But that seems so far away to most of us. What we really need is something closer and more tangible. Like friends.

Recently a few good friends decided to try friendship-based accountability for their giving. They made a pact that begins, "We desire to follow God and invite each other to hold us accountable in the way we use our resources. . . . We will be open and honest with each other, seeking to provide counsel and encouragement to align our hearts and our wallets."

They actually open their books to each other, inviting questions and feedback. It's like getting a free and recurring audit, minus the threat of penalties and prison. Sound scary? A little awkward? Don't knock it until you've tried it. These friends are finding impetus to budget more wisely and give more generously, while also experiencing joy and camaraderie in the process.

Send Your Heart Soaring

Jesus said, "Where your treasure is, there your heart will be also" (Matthew 6:21). If that's true, where is your heart? It might be in your garage, in your house or in your investment portfolio. We place our money in the things we value, and our hearts follow.

Most of us have earthbound hearts, but you can send your heart to a more secure location: above the sun, "where moths and vermin do not destroy, and thieves do not break in and steal" (Matthew 6:20). This runs counter to the classic midlife temptations to grab things we've not yet had the chance to enjoy: the sports car, the second home, the boat, the season tickets. When we were young and idealistic, those things felt excessive. But by our forties, we've mastered the art of rationalization—like the friend who said he felt a little check in his spirit before buying the Audi, then added with a chuckle, "But I got over it!"

The temptation is that other people are indulging, so I will too. I mean, if not now, when?

This calls for wisdom, because the truth is that God "richly provides us with everything for our enjoyment" (1 Timothy 6:17). Often midlife affords us the opportunity to enjoy at least a few of the things we weren't in a position to experience before. But bear in mind that those words, spoken by Paul to Timothy, are directed at rich people, not as a license to indulge but as a challenge to give: the whole world is yours to enjoy—so give as you've been given to.

Like Qoheleth, Paul would say that the joy of the new car depreciates as fast as the value of the vehicle itself. The boat becomes "a hole in the water." And the vacation home takes you away from church and community most weekends, because now that you have it, you've got to get your money's worth. That's why Paul adds that through generosity the rich "lay up treasure for themselves as a firm foundation for the coming age, so that they may take hold of the life that is truly life" (1 Timothy 6:19).

Taking hold of the life that is truly life—isn't that what we all want in midlife? We want something more thrilling than we're currently experiencing. We want some of that you-only-go-around-once gusto immortalized in the old beer commercial.

Take heed! *Life that is truly life* is not something you can buy your way into. It's something you can give your way into.

In light of eternity, what would it look like if we had an "above the sun" perspective on money? I (Peter) have good friends, George and Courtney, who were on the brink of several lucrative deals that would make them financially secure and free to enjoy all the pleasures the world can offer. But reading Scripture and understanding their own hearts, they knew wealth is a snare that can grab the unsuspecting heart and never let it go. They didn't want that to happen. So in their thirties, they drew up a contract to cap their lifestyle at a dramatically lower level than they could have chosen. They understood that the patterns they established at that crucial time would impact the rest of their lives, and they wanted to live differently.

At the beginning of the contract, they wrote, "We desire to live within a conservative budget—no matter what our financial situation may be. We resolve that this should always be the case and we memorialize our intent in this 'Contract' so that, come what may in the years ahead, we would not depart from this objective."

George told me that when he signed the contract, he wept. Why? "It was an overwhelming joy of aligning our actions with a deeper kind of desire, the desire for Christ and his Kingdom."

His emotion was the polar opposite of the stress most people feel with regard to money. He had discovered the joy in the promise of Hebrews 13:5:

> Keep your lives free from the love of money and be content with what you have, because God has said,
>
> "Never will I leave you;
>   never will I forsake you."

As you peer through the fog of midlife financial issues, remember that your faith is not in your 401(k) but in your Father's provision. Midlife offers a unique opportunity to readjust your perspective, to cap your lifestyle and to uncork your generosity.

(UN)REST

How Do You Stop and Rest Before Life Stops You?

Hurry is not of the devil; hurry is the devil.

CARL JUNG

An October fog hangs thick outside my window. With mere weeks remaining before this manuscript is due, I (Peter) am driven from bed to desk by the deadline, hoping for some early-morning inspiration.

I need it quickly. In a few minutes, a bleary-eyed, bed-headed child will walk in. Next thing you know, I'll be pouring cereal and wrestling kids into semi-matching clothes. Then it's off to a birthday party, my son's flag football game and dinner with our small group. When the sun sets and my kids are tucked back into bed, I'll be here at my computer again, working on a donor proposal due first thing Monday morning.

Laurel is away for the weekend. How does she do this job every day?

Busyness is a hallmark of modern life. It's paraded in our culture as if a busy life is equivalent to a productive one. If you listen carefully, you'll hear the boast beneath people's busyness. A calendar full of commitments is like a Girl Scout's sash full of merit badges. It makes us feel important. *If I weren't so necessary, I wouldn't be stretched so thin.*

Midlife is the busiest season of them all. We tend to think the busiest is the preschool years, with its 24/7 childcare. But wait until those kids have schedules of their own and both parents work. There is *never* enough time.

Wasn't technology supposed to help with this? It once held the promise of a more reasonable pace—a four-day workweek even. Instead, my phone is the first thing I touch in the morning, as I use it as an alarm. I push one icon and go to my inbox before I go to the bathroom. I push another and start sending vital text messages to my colleagues. (By the way, has it ever bothered you that we call these buttons *icons*, which are historically items of worship?)

You may remember the olden days when Blackberry controlled the PDA market. That's when we started living heads down and thumbs up. We engaged in public displays of affection with our personal digital assistants. People started calling them Crackberries. But as it turns out, they were just the gateway drug to more addictive technologies.

We suffer from digiphrenia—a term coined to describe how technology "encourages us to be in more than one place at the same time."[1] And it's not working. In our effort not to miss anything, we often miss everything.

We rise early, log in, caffeinate and multitask all day long. Sometime near the end of the cycle, we feel exhausted, but our minds don't shut down. Thank the good Lord for sleep aids.

A few years back, Peter and I (Greg) were traveling together to a conference in Atlanta. We stopped at a grocery store before checking into our hotel because I had forgotten my "meds." I quickly found them: a six-pack of 5-Hour Energy and a bottle of Tylenol PM. Before ringing me up, the clerk just looked at me sympathetically.

We know that this harried lifestyle has many consequences. The bags under my eyes are just two of them. But I don't have time to think about that. There is a deadline approaching and emails that need responses.

Superstitiously Super-Busy

The wise heart will know the proper time and procedure.

ECCLESIASTES 8:5

The behavioral psychologist B. F. Skinner put hungry pigeons in a cage and rigged up a mechanism to dispense food pellets at regular intervals. The pigeons, of course, didn't know this. They just saw food magically appearing, which they eagerly ate.

So, what did the birds do during the interval between snacks? Sit around and do bird things? *No.* It turns out pigeons are superstitious. Whatever they were doing just prior to the food appearing, they counted as *causing* the food to appear. So they began engaging in all sorts of bizarre, ritualistic behavior.

Did a bird just happen to turn left before receiving the food? Suddenly it started turning counterclockwise in dizzying circles until the next pellet came. Did the bird just happen to bob its head before being fed? Soon it was head banging like a rock star.

Understand: the food was coming at a particular time, no matter what the birds did. But the birds thought their frenzied behavior made it happen. It's a different twist on the old insanity definition. But in this case, it's doing the same thing expecting *the same* results. Or doing the same thing *because we're absolutely convinced it causes* the same results.

I wonder how often God looks down and thinks our behavior is for the birds. Maybe that's why Jesus said, "So do not worry, saying, 'What shall we eat?' or 'What shall we drink?' or 'What shall we wear?'

For the pagans run after all these things, and your heavenly Father knows that you need them" (Matthew 6:31-32). God dispenses his blessings at regular intervals, whether we dance or not. He provides for his children right on time.

But we've fallen into a pattern of ritualistic rushing that we think is continuing to pay the bills and sustain our lives. Sure, there are some responsibilities we need to attend to. The paycheck won't come if we don't show up at work five days a week. But many of the other habits we've acquired are utterly irrelevant but supremely exhausting.

Some people receive a gift in midlife that proves the point. That gift comes in the form of a heart attack. Or unemployment. Or burnout. A crisis strikes that brings all the hurry to a halt. We're sidelined, and we think the jig is surely up.

But then something amazing happens. We slow down and rest. We think. We get back into our right minds. We deactivate that reactive "reptilian brain" at the back of our heads and engage the rational cortex up front. Priorities are reassessed; some habits change. We bring the rpms back under the red line. Eventually we get back to work, but we do it in a different mode. We establish better boundaries and protect our time at home. The tension leaves our necks. We smile more. We may even get a promotion.

Of course, we don't need to pay such a high tuition to learn these lessons. It doesn't require a layoff or a health scare. We can make the changes now, of our own accord, before they're foisted upon us. Midlife is a time to reconsider how we want to live for the rest of our lives.

Both of us have quite a few employees, and they are valuable to us personally and organizationally. Every once in a while, one of them steps into our office and levels with us, saying, "I'm dying over here. I need some help." And you know what our first CEO reaction is? It's not: "How can I get rid of you and find someone who won't complain?" It's simply this: "How can I help you? We would much rather strategize a sustainable life with you than replace you." We can't vouch for your boss, but that's how we see it.

Of course, there may be quite a bit of hurry in your life that isn't even work related. *You* are the boss of that. So put on your CEO hat and offer yourself some help.

Exhaustion Is Expensive

We've seen some massive manmade disasters in our lifetime, including the Exxon Valdez oil spill and the nuclear meltdowns at Three Mile Island and Chernobyl. A common cause of each of these—and many others—was exhaustion. Overly tired people had delayed responses and made poor decisions. How many of us have our own spills and meltdowns looming?

Lack of sleep is strongly linked to depression, forgetfulness, lack of sex drive (yes, that can melt down too) and increased likelihood of heart disease, heart attack, stroke and diabetes. Studies also tell us that people who sleep less than six hours a day are almost "30 percent more likely to become obese than those who slept seven to nine hours."[2]

As I (Peter) travel internationally, I'm reminded that not everyone lives in perpetual motion. In many cultures, tasks are not as important as relationships. So we sit for tea and conversation. We greet everyone when entering a room. We pack less into our days, because we know we need margin for unexpected conversations. In Swahili, the word for white man, *muzungu*, means "the one who spins around." Africans have seen too many Americans act like Skinner's pigeons.

Aren't we supposed to burn out instead of rust out? That's certainly our culture's value. But it's killing us. And in the quiet hours of an early morning or in the stillness of a late night, I long to detox. I need to get clean.

A few people seem to hang on the other side of the pendulum, slipping into acedia, a state of apathy and listnessness. It's what monks call the "noonday demon,"[3] and it leads to sloth. Those falling into this need a kick off the couch. As Qoheleth wrote,

> Through laziness, the rafters sag
>> because of idle hands, the house leaks. (Ecclesiastes 10:18)

Boredom is just as dangerous as busyness. But since sloth is less common in midlife, let's focus on the more common problem.

Life Is Too Short to Live So Fast

A certain logic suggests that given our vapor-short lives, it makes sense to hurry. We have only so many precious days and minutes, so cram as much into them as possible. But no matter how busy we make ourselves, there will never be enough time. The quantity of life is finite and largely beyond our control. But quality is within our grasp.

Sheldon Vanauken was an American author and friend of C. S. Lewis best known for his autobiography *A Severe Mercy*, which reflects upon his wife's death. In one passage, he laments the pressure of time, expressing that he could have done more to maximize the quality of his experiences with his wife while she lived.

> I saw with immense clarity that we had always been harried by time. All our dreams back there in Glenmerle had come true: the schooner *Grey Goose* under the wind, the far islands of Hawaii in the dark-blue rolling Pacific, the spires of Oxford. But all the fulfillments were somehow, it seemed to me, incomplete, temporary, *hurried.* We wished to know, to savor, to sink in— into the heart of the experience—to possess it wholly. But there was never enough time; something still eluded us . . . there was more, something still deeper, that we hadn't time enough— world and time enough—to reach. We didn't at all feel that we were *unable* to reach it, only that there wasn't time enough.[4]

He goes on to write of their dream to one day return to the islands of Hawaii and try to take it all in, but he knows "if we had gone back, there wouldn't have been time enough then, either, for ahead there would be a terminus. Always."[5]

I (Greg) relate to his frustration. A few years ago, my wife and I took a bucket-list trip to Israel with another couple. Despite the cautions of others who had been there, we crammed as much into our nine days as possible. The wise counsel had been, "Be selective. You can't see it all, so don't even try. Choose a limited number of sites, and linger at them. Take your Bibles. Be still. You can go back again sometime and get what you missed."

Bah! Some people are so soft! We rejected the spiritual retreat and went for the whirlwind tour.

Not that we zipped through everything, but we did bite off more than necessary. In hindsight, my favorite spot was by the Huldah Gates at the Temple Mount, where Pentecost broke out and three thousand new Christians were baptized. Most people skip that spot entirely, but we spent two hours there, much of it in quiet. It was one of the places where, in the words of Vanauken, I "sank into the heart of the experience."[6]

But we blow through so much of life, especially the routine days, with precious little appreciation. As Vanauken writes, "In the reality of Now, the clock is always ticking."[7] We're always thinking about the next task, the next project, the next goal.

The Happiness of Hurrylessness

> *Who is like the wise?*
> *Who knows the explanation of things?*
> *A person's wisdom brightens their face*
> *and changes its hard appearance.*

> Ecclesiastes 8:1-2

John Ortberg, pastor of Menlo Park Presbyterian Church, once asked Christian philosopher Dallas Willard about the key to spiritual health. He describes Willard's response:

> [There was a] long pause.
>
> "You must ruthlessly eliminate hurry from your life," he said at last.
>
> Another long pause.
>
> "Okay, I've written that one down," I told him, a little impatiently. "That's a good one. Now what else is there?" I had many things to do, and this was a long-distance call, so I was anxious to cram as many units of spiritual wisdom into the least amount of time possible.
>
> Another long pause.
>
> "There is nothing else," he said. "You must ruthlessly eliminate hurry from your life."[8]

In the Bible, hurry is often associated with wickedness.

- It is the wicked whose feet *rush* to do evil. (Proverbs 6:18)
- They are *swift* to shed blood. (Proverbs 1:16)
- They make *haste* and miss the way. (Proverbs 19:2)
- They are *quick* to quarrel. (Proverbs 20:3)
- They *run* even when no one pursues. (Leviticus 26:17)

In other words, Willard knows of what he speaks. A restless life wounds others and ruins us. A restful life refreshes both others and us. Psalm 46:10 says, "Be still, and know that I am God."

Several years ago, Shelly, a single mom in my (Greg's) church felt convicted because she was hurrying to find a new husband. She knew she was forcing the issue and decided to slow down and let God be God. She wrote to me,

> I closed my online dating profile last week. In addition to the

time it was taking to reply to emails and meet people, the bottom
line is that none of the guys had the potential of being "my guy,"
and I knew it. I was trying to make something happen instead of
trusting my God to bring my guy into my life. After making this
decision, I have had such clarity. I am creating the family experiences I've always wanted, and there's no guy required. The kids
and I had Family Fun Day last week, which culminated with a
"private showing" of *The Princess Bride* in a fort that took up the
entire living room. I've also been able to generate some serious
momentum in my business, and it's only been a week.

Hurrylessness enabled her to "sink into the heart of the experience," both with her kids and with her job. The family time was
richer, and the work time more productive.

It creates richer, more productive times with God too. When
frenzied, if we pray at all, we make perfunctory requests for blessing.
We superstitiously bob our heads into our Bibles for a quick peck, then
do a ritual prayer turn before dinner. That's spirituality for the birds.

The philosopher Blaise Pascal spoke of it this way:

> I have often said that the sole cause of man's unhappiness is
> that he does not know how to stay quietly in his room. . . .
> What people want is not the easy peaceful life that allows us
> to think of our unhappy condition, nor the dangers of war, nor
> the burdens of office, but the agitation that takes our mind off
> of it and diverts us. That is why we prefer the hunt to the
> capture. That is why men are so fond of hustle and bustle; that
> is why prison is such a fearful punishment; that is why the
> pleasures of solitude are so incomprehensible.[9]

The first word of Hebrew worship is *hear.* "Hear, O Israel: the
LORD our God, the LORD is one" (Deuteronomy 6:4). God's people
live not by eating but by hearing. They live not by bread alone but

by every word that comes out of God's mouth (8:3). Paul carries this into the New Testament, saying, "Consequently faith comes from hearing the message, and the message is heard through the word about Christ" (Romans 10:17).

How well do you hear when you're in a hurry?

Good listening is always associated with stillness. You stop, turn down the volume, look into a person's face and actively acknowledge that she is speaking to you.

In college, I (Greg) was first taught the discipline of silence. Not the kind where you go days without speaking—as helpful as that can be—but the kind where you go moments without speaking. I was taught to read my Bible, listen to the text, pray the text and then listen again—a form of the classic practice *lectio divina*. I was taught to start and finish in silence and to end my devotional times by saying, "God, is there something else you want to say to me today?"

I can't say that I do that every day, but it's a regular part of my discipline that serves me well. It's like lingering in the shower or going for a long run; it's where I get some of my best insights and ideas. I ask God if he has anything to add, any other thoughts to share, any additional guidance to offer. We have a God who speaks; the question is whether anyone is listening.

Breaking the Addiction

Most of us don't need convincing that we're addicted to busyness. We know it. We feel it. We know we've been living from moment to moment, never fully *in the moment*, incapable of being fully present. Douglas Rushkoff observes, "Our society has reoriented itself to the present moment. Everything is live, real time and always-on."[10] He calls it "present shock," saying it's not just that we speed things up but that we diminish everything that isn't hap-pening right now. And that's no way to live.

So in the middle of the midlife rush, how do we find the gift of stillness? The solution begins by diagnosing the root of your busyness. *What drives you so much?* Is your frenetic pace a discomfort with silence? Is it a mad dash for an idolatrous desire? Or is it a juvenile attempt to prove yourself to yourself, to your family or to God?

J.D. Greear encourages people to simply pray,

> In Christ, there is nothing I can do that would make you love me more and nothing I have done that makes you love me less. Your presence and approval are all I need for everlasting joy. As you have been to me, so I will be to others. As I pray, I'll measure your compassion by the cross and your power by the resurrection.[11]

That's the kind of centering prayer that can help you both work hard and rest in peace (even before you die).

Midlife is an invitation to go beyond diagnosing the problem in order to focus on what ultimately matters—and perhaps to find new freedom in saying no. Warren Buffet famously wrote, "The difference between successful people and really successful people is that really successful people say no to almost everything."[12]

If we want to be "really successful" in matters of supreme importance, we have to ensure we don't say yes to every invitation. Practically, this means I don't accept any new opportunity without waiting twenty-four hours. This buffer allows me to consider if it's truly a priority. Second, for every yes, there must be a corresponding no. What will I decline in order to compensate for this added responsibility?

Managing your schedule is kind of like managing your closet. It's best practice that for every new item you get, you rid yourself of an old one. Similarly, rather than overstuffing your calendar, understand that every yes must contain a no. It's the only way to maintain some sanity and balance. If you have no time to serve others or to be with your kids (chauffeuring doesn't count), you're too busy.

Midlife is the time to narrow your focus. To say no to the clubs and activities you don't really enjoy. To coach one sport and not three. To get off those boards where you're not adding value. At this point in your life, your not-to-do list is every bit as important as your to-do list.

You might even try saying some noes to your kids. In my (Greg's) family, we always had a general rule of one sport or extracurricular per kid at a time. Nowadays, every activity wants to be all-consuming anyway, so who has time for more? And we never budged with regard to Sundays. That was God's day and ours. If a sport wanted that time, that sport wasn't for us.

We need discipline, resolve and a little imagination to work, love, pray and rest in midlife. So choose wisely, and don't be bullied into more than you can handle. Everyone will thank you for it.

And we love Bob Goff's mischievous advice: "Quit something every Thursday."

AGE(LESS)

How Do We Grow Up Gracefully?

I am tarred and feathered with Time.

Ogden Nash

A few years ago, I (Peter) was looking at pictures from a Fourth of July picnic with my family. I came across a shot of my children seated with some guy who had his back to the camera. He was balding, middle-aged and a little suspicious looking, the way he was cozying up to my family.

"Who is that?" I asked my wife.

"Honey, that's *you*!" she responded.

Noooo!

I couldn't believe it. It couldn't be me. That guy in the picture was missing hair—and a fair amount of it. It had to be some transient party crasher, not the guy I look at in the mirror every morning.

Without saying a word, I dashed upstairs for a review. I grabbed a mirror, turned around and stared at the top of my head, where I saw the indisputable visual evidence. My wife was right. The play stood as called. For the first time, I knew what everybody else probably had known for a long time.

Facing the brutal facts, I began looking for ways to fight the erosion. Rogaine, plugs, weaves, the comb-over. I even stumbled upon a toupee website. Who knew there were so many options? But they all came with significant downsides, and despite the promises of the advertisers, none looked natural.

A few months later, I was comparing hairlines with my friend Sparky and asked if he'd tried Propecia. "Yes," he said, "but it had terrible side effects on another, more important part of my body."

"What about Rogaine?" I inquired, hopeful.

"Nope. Ineffective. I'm screwed."

We're all at different stages of thinning, sagging, wrinkling and spider veining. Nothing is more obsessed over through the middle years than our physical appearance. And if we don't have the wherewithal to change our body itself, we can at least adorn it differently. A leather jacket and three-day shadow can morph any middle-aged dude into his former bad self. Or so we think. (Tip of the day: leather is usually a sure sign that you're trying too hard.)

On facing forty, Jen Hatmaker wrote, "We are sorry to disclose this, young ones, but you can no longer quit eating bread for one day and lose six pounds. I know this is hard. I once believed that, for the rest of my life, if I made minor adjustments and took a jog, those tight jeans would fit by Tuesday. Your body is over this by forty. It just wants to be fat and happy."[1]

But like the drowning man struggling for one last breath, we make one last desperate grasp to get our former bodies back. In 2012, people living in America spent $11 billion on facelifts, Botox injections, breast augmentations and various other aesthetic procedures.[2] In our overly photographed day, the pressure only increases. According to industry experts, selfies have led to a rise in plastic surgery. A third of plastic surgeons say their clients seek help because of their appearance in social media.[3]

Author Jennifer Weiner writes, "Show me a body part, I'll show you someone who's making money by telling women that theirs looks wrong and they need to fix it. Tone it, work it out, tan it, bleach it, tattoo it, lipo it, remove all the hair, lose every bit of jiggle."[4] Even kids fall prey. So many youth are using Botox that some call it "teen toxing."[5]

I had dinner with a harpist who played at "Botox parties" in California. She strummed as the clients, like heroin addicts, took their next injections. Hearing about it, her father commented, "People can get face jobs, but the real problem is between their ears."

Not Without a Fight

Most of us won't go to such extremes, but we're still determined not to go down without a fight. I (Greg) was a slender distance runner for twenty years: five ten, a buck fifty. Entering midlife, I proudly weighed the same as I did in high school. Many would envy that fact, but for me, slenderness came with a downside. Thinner people wrinkle faster, and I was doing that rapidly. The crevices on my face were as long as my training runs. Still, I consoled myself with the fact that I could run farther and faster than most of my peers.

Then one day my colleague Andy brought some friends to a Sunday service. As I got up to speak, one of them leaned over and whispered, "Is he a runner?"

"Yeah," my coworker replied.

"I knew it," the friend said, "he's got that gaunt, emaciated look."

And that's the day I became a disciple of Tony Horton. Gaunt and emaciated? *Not for long.* I got P90X, pressed "play" religiously and ingested prodigious amounts of protein. Over the next few months, I added size and definition, filling my shirts with twenty more pounds of *me* than I used to carry. And people noticed. I regularly received compliments, and people wanted to know my secret.

Sadly I'm sure I converted more people to Tony Horton that year than to Jesus Christ. And what was I teaching about the priorities of life? Verbally I kept teaching the Bible, but I think people perceived different values. I'm called to model godliness, but people noticed buffness. I'm called to let people see my progress in spiritual matters (1 Timothy 4:15), but my physical gains were much more noticeable.

Subtle dark forces were at work. I was succumbing to the spirit of the age—and worse, sanctifying it with my pastoral persona.

Now, I don't think there's anything wrong with working out. In fact, stewarding your body with a healthy diet and exercise is a good thing. But somebody has to model a sense of priority and pro- portion. "Physical training is of some value," Paul said, "but god- liness has value for all things, holding promise for both the present life and the life to come" (1 Timothy 4:8).

But most of us are more religious about our bodies than our souls. We take supplements, apply balms and adhere to rigorous training regimens, all in an attempt to keep things lifted, taut and attractive. But when it's all said and done, the winner and still un- defeated heavyweight champion of the world is . . . gravity.

That leads to midlife disillusionment—which is a good thing. Who wants to live under illusions? We *will* age. We *are aging.* And even when we make radical midlife "improvements," the before- and-after pictures don't tell the whole story. We forget that there is always an after-the-after picture. The body looks great, but the soul looks emaciated.

The Downside of Youth

You who are young, be happy while you are young,
and let your heart give you joy in the days of your youth.

Follow the ways of your heart
and whatever your eyes see,
but know that for all these things
God will bring you into judgment.
So then, banish anxiety from your heart
and cast off the troubles of your body,
for youth and vigor are meaningless.

ECCLESIASTES 11:9-10

Beyond their tight bodies and full heads of hair, young people often have passion that we midlifers feel waning in ourselves. So Qoheleth's endorses the enjoyment of life while we're capable. The world is full of shiny, desirable things, so follow your heart. "Follow the ways of your heart and whatever your eyes see," the Teacher encourages above.

But that's a very tricky way to walk. It's a tightrope. On the one side, you don't want to fall off into radical asceticism or priggish fundamentalism, as if rejecting life's good things was itself good. No, good things are meant to be relished with gratitude. But on the other hand, you don't want to fall off into carnal self-gratification, which, in the end, makes desires uppermost and miscasts good things as *ultimate* goods.

And that's the propensity we all have. Just about the time you embrace some pleasure as a good gift of God, you begin idolizing it. Creator and creation get flipped, and a once justifiable thing becomes the ground for divine discipline. That's what the Teacher drives at when he says that for all these things God will bring you to judgment. Passion is a good thing, but unredeemed, under-the-sun passion is not. So enjoy—but be prepared to take your lumps.

Hasn't that been your experience?

God hardwired his world with consequences, both natural and spiritual. And we've all run afoul of them. You enjoy the party but suffer the hangover. You revel in the moment but regret the aftereffects. And people split fifty/fifty over whether it was all worth it.

But most wise people look back on their youth and admit they would do some things differently. The momentary pleasures didn't outweigh the long-term consequences.

Yet given the opportunity to go back, who would? We barely escaped middle school with our lives, and high school jealousies ripped us apart. Who wants to volunteer for another round of hormonal heartbreak? Who wants another dose of AP World History? I'll keep my mature station in life, thank you very much. To chase youth would be as pointless as driving a thousand miles an hour to chase the setting sun. Your life would always be "day," but would you call that "living in the light"?

The Downside of Age

Don't worry. It's downside time, but upside's a-comin'.

> *Remember your Creator*
> *in the days of your youth,*
> *before the days of trouble come*
> *and the years approach when you will say,*
> *"I find no pleasure in them"—*
> *before the sun and the light*
> *and the moon and the stars grow dark,*
> *and the clouds return after the rain;*
> *when the keepers of the house tremble,*
> *and the strong men stoop,*
> *when the grinders cease because they are few,*
> *and those looking through the windows grow dim;*
> *when the doors to the street are closed*
> *and the grinding fades;*
> *when the people rise up at the sound of birds,*
> *but all their songs grow faint;*
> *when people are afraid of heights*

> *and of dangers in the streets;*
> *when the almond tree blossoms*
> *and the grasshopper drags itself along*
> *and desire no longer is stirred.*
> *Then people go to their eternal home*
> *and mourners go about the streets.*

ECCLESIASTES 12:1-5

In a doleful piece of poetry, Qoheleth describes the aging process. It's beautiful writing if you like Nietzsche and dress goth. It's an ode to our unmaking.

Many people see this passage as an allegorical description of the aging process. The sun, moon and stars darken just as eyes fail. The grinders—the teeth—stop working, because they are few. The almond tree blossoms into a head of white hair, and grasshopper bellies lop out over waistlines. (Does "clouds return after the rain" mean we have to go to the bathroom more often?) And who doesn't rue the day when "desire is no longer stirred." That's the capper to this poem and the nadir of life as we know it.

Very sobering.

A few years ago I (Greg) interviewed some of the senior matriarchs of our church—women who have bolstered the ministry for half a century with their faithful service and prayer. They have been the great constants of our growing, changing congregation. True saints.

Most of them have known tremendous hardship. They've lived through war and depression, surgeries and emergencies of every kind. They've lost loved ones, both spouses and children. But they carry themselves with such grace and mature love. So as we talked about the trials of aging, I asked, "Given all that you've lived through, does it get easier to trust God as you get older?"

Immediately one of the two Ruths on the panel said, "No, it gets harder."

That's it? *Gee, thanks, St. Ruth.* I wanted her to say that insecurities fade and confidence soars in old age. But I had to appreciate her honesty. In their eighties and nineties, these women are still fighting the good fight of faith. But it's a fight, and apparently it never stops being one.

That reminds me of a conversation I had recently with our children's staff. As the four of us ate lunch, we recognized that we spanned four decades, from the twenties to the fifties. (I am finding more and more that I represent the oldsters.) We somehow got onto the topic of our insecurities, the two younger staffers sharing how eager they were to "finally grow up" and get past them. That's when we older ones said, "Um, you know what? You might want to just go ahead and make peace with those insecurities, because we pretty much have the same ones now that we had twenty years ago."

And that's what I like to call paying it forward.

Insecurity is no respecter of persons. It doesn't matter who you are, how old you are or how much you got it goin' on. In 2012, supermodel Cameron Russell gave a TED talk on what it's really like to be a model. Her words were insightful and self-revealing. Turns out it's hard to look perfect, and in more ways than one.

> I am insecure. And I'm insecure because I have to think about what I look like every day. If you're wondering, "if I have thinner thighs or shinier hair, will I be happier?" you just need to meet a group of models. They have the thinnest thighs and the shiniest hair and the coolest clothes and they're the most physically insecure people probably on the planet.[6]

By our cultural standards, Russell is a standard-bearer for beauty. She's tall and thin with flowing brown hair and flawless skin. But good looks can't secure a soul. The fact that she would say it must've made God proud.

Look on the Bright Side of Life

So, what are we to do? Qoheleth says, "Remember your Creator." Do it in the days of your youth and do it in the days of your maturity. And focus on that title: Creator.

While Ecclesiastes 12 may well describe the aging process, some Bible scholars don't see the text's meaning exhausted there. They see it pointing to bigger, broader realities. They see it alluding to the world's demise and rebirth. Qoheleth employs apocalyptic language, especially when speaking of the sun, moon and stars being darkened. Several prophets use this same imagery as the key sign of the Day of the Lord's Wrath, the great upheaval at the end of this age when the whole world will pass through the fires of judgment.

As frightening as that prospect is, it's not all doom and gloom. There's a brilliant silver lining because, taking the whole apocalyptic storyline into account, we remember that after the Creator un-creates, he re-creates. He gives us all what we hope for most.

Currently the whole globe groans, insecure in its present state, yearning for a redeemed one. It groans just as we groan, insecure in these frail bodies but yearning for immortal ones. And God promises to give them. The apostle Paul wrote, "If the Spirit of him who raised Jesus from the dead is living in you, he who raised Christ from the dead will also give life to your mortal bodies because of his Spirit who lives in you" (Romans 8:11; also see the entire chapter).

We can't remind people enough that the future is an embodied one. Heaven is not wispy souls lounging on clouds, playing harps. It's physical and earthly. Granted, the biblical picture of the afterlife is your soul in heaven while your body lies dead in the ground. But there's an after-the-after picture when that body—along with all of creation—is resurrected.

When you see above the sun, you realize how silly it is to fight a losing battle with your body when the Creator has already fought a winning battle for it.

The Age of Opportunity

What a gift it is to grow old. To see more of the world. To extend your productive years. To watch children and grandchildren grow to full maturity. To witness God's plan unfold over longer periods. Physical aging is the price of admission into these experiences.

Most countries have life expectancies far shorter than the United States average of seventy-nine. Several African countries have a life expectancy of less than fifty. But while few countries have life spans as long and healthy as ours, many view old age in a healthier way. In South Korea, they throw big parties for sixtieth and seventieth birthdays. The sixtieth birthday is known as the *hwan-gap*, and it's largely a celebration of the fact that modern medicine has enabled individuals to outlive their ancestors. To top it, the seventieth birthday is known as the *kohCui*, meaning "old and rare."[7]

On the island of Sardinia, off the coast of Italy, the Province of Nuoro contains one of the highest concentrations of centenarians in the world. And what is the secret to the longevity of their population? According to explorer and educator Dan Buettner, it's the way they respect the elderly.[8] So let's do both the elderly and ourselves a favor: respect old age now, and maybe it will become even more respectable by the time we get there.

As Proverbs 16:31 reminds us, "Gray hair is a crown of splendor." And many cultures don't bestow real leadership or responsibility until you show some of it. Fine wine, cars, buildings, music and *people* grow better with age. And maybe midlife allows us to make peace with our aging bodies and to count wisdom as the real indicator of our wellness. The former supermodel Paulina Porizkova shared a remarkable perspective in her midforties:

> To me, to let yourself age means that you're comfortable with who you are. . . . The beauty of age was supposed to be about

the wisdom acquired and with it, an acceptance and celebration of who you are. Now all we want for people to see is
that we have not yet attained that wisdom. Aging has become
something to fight, not something to accept.[9]

Love Handles

In midlife, it's time to make concrete decisions to impact our
health positively. You have this one-and-only body, and what you
did with it in college is not what you should do with it today.
Pulling all-nighters: not a good idea. Eating the whole bag of
Doritos: not a good idea. Bodysurfing at a concert: definitely not
a good idea.

A little more love will make your body last long and help it
embody the wisdom that will be your calling card later in life. So
consider how you will care for your brain, body and soul, because,
as one doctor commented, "Up to age forty, you had a free ride.
Now it's time to work for your health."[10]

Brain. Recent neuroscience shows that our minds can continue
to grow at any age. There is evidence our brains have the ability to
change throughout life, which is called brain plasticity or neuro-
genesis. It's no longer assumed that connections in the brain became
fixed as we age. Nor is it inevitable that we lose brain cells.

To the contrary, aging "does *not* always lead to a pronounced decline and loss of cognitive ability. Much to the contrary, many older
adults live a creative and productive life to the end. . . . Cell processes,
such as synapses and axons, also change. Yet these changes may
represent yet another fine-tuning of our cerebral networks, as we
gain more patience, forbearance and wisdom with age."[11]

Practically speaking, that may mean doing more than Sudoku.
Start studying that language you've always wanted to learn. Get Ro-
setta Stone and get after it; hey, in midlife you can probably afford it.

Take guitar lessons. Read substantive books. Take a class, or pursue another degree. Write.

Body. If you haven't worked out in about a decade, start, but take it easy. Ecclesiastes 1:9 proclaims that there's nothing new under the sun, and that is particularly true when it comes to the basics of body health: Get your heart rate up. Drink water. Eat more plants. Go to bed at a regular hour, and get some sleep.

And there is always new research pointing out the benefits of ancient, forgotten practices. Like standing. Humans used to stand a lot. We did manual labor and spent hours a day on our feet. Now we sit in couches, cars and offices. Some studies are now showing that standing more can be a bigger boon to health and longevity than exercise programs.[12]

Based on that fact, a couple of my coworkers and I (Greg) added computer stands to our offices, so we can stand to work. I still do my extreme workouts (despite the fact that I have less and less of a beach body), and I like knowing that I'm helping my body even when I'm mostly working with my mind.

And don't forget the benefits of being healthy together. My neighbor and his wife walk together every day. Various people from our church make up half the clientele at a local CrossFit. And my wife runs religiously with her "Fit and Fifty" friends (as we like to call them). Nothing gets you off your duff and out the door like knowing other people are waiting for you.

My (Peter's) friend Kent Annan celebrated his fortieth birthday by participating in a Tough Mudder, which is an intense obstacle run that ranges from ten to twelve miles in length. Working in teams, runners crawl under barbed wire, dive into freezing water and run through hanging live electrical wires. It's more than a physical challenge; it also tests mental strength and stamina.

Kent raised the bar on his health and also raised money for Haiti Partners, the nonprofit where he serves as codirector. Instead of fortieth birthday presents, he asked people to help sponsor children in Haiti. He shared this with *Christianity Today*:

> Exercise is an act of stewardship with two primary aims: to care for our bodies so we can give them more readily to the loving service of God and neighbor, and to enjoy our bodies as the divine gifts they are. Of course, our bodies can also fail and betray us—I'm partly doing the Tough Mudder because of my family history of heart disease. Vigorous exercise should raise my good HDL cholesterol. I need my body and spirit to help each other along.[13]

Soul. It's easy to obsess over mind and body while leaving the soul untouched. That's a big mistake, because while we live *in* our bodies, we live *out of* our souls. The soul is the core, the command center.

The apostle Paul reminded his good friends that he put no confidence in the flesh. And if anyone could have, it was Paul. He had a "body of work," a physical pedigree, like few others. But the fleshly things about Paul meant nothing to him because they meant nothing to God. Rather, he had a soulish desire to know Christ. To commune with him. To become like him in dying to self. (See Philippians 3:1-14.)

However, often our overweening attention to our bodies is nothing less than living for self. My (Greg's) wife, Deane, is a model of wholeness and balance in the body-and-soul department. She's a runner, and a pretty good one. She competes well in her age group because of good genes and routines. But there's no question that her spiritual disciplines are even more important. You can find Deane every morning, without fail, sitting at the dining room table with an open Bible and a cup of chai. As with physical exercise, she understands that there's really "nothing new under the sun." You crack the Book and you read it. You feed and exercise your soul.

And that makes her one of the wisest, most solid people I know. As the old saying goes, "A Bible that's falling apart is usually owned by a person who isn't."

Ageless Wisdom

I (Peter) recently visited Haddon Robinson in a local nursing home. This deeply respected pastor and theologian is a modern giant of the faith. But when we met his voice was quiet, not like the powerful voice I'd heard in so many sermons. Parkinson's disease was taking its toll. He shuffled more than walked through the salad bar line. Bypassing the steak and potatoes, I followed his lead in piling my plate with greens.

When I asked him about his current activities, he commented, "I can no longer preach," but then he went on to share about the conversations he was having with others at the home and the organizations with which he remained active. As our lunch progressed, he offered insights on navigating life, career and love. I leaned in, deeply impacted by his words of wisdom.

His body was frail, but his spirit was strong. His feet shuffled, but his heart had not grown weary in doing good. Outwardly he was wasting away; inwardly he was renewed day by day (2 Corinthians 4:16).

I want to end like that, waxing large of soul, using each breath to point people above the sun until I fall into the arms of Christ.

9

(DIS)CONNECTED

How Do We Break Midlife's Isolation to Find Authentic Friendship?

We are broken persons and live in broken communities in a state of brokenness. We do not readily fit together. We are like a bunch of porcupines trying to huddle together for warmth, who are always driven apart out of the fear we can inflict on each other with our quills.

BASIL PENNINGTON

In the 2002 movie *About a Boy*, Hugh Grant plays Will Freeman, a single, early-middle-aged slacker who lives luxuriously off the royalties of a Christmas song written by his deceased father. He's a solitary man with a single life priority: himself. (Hence the name Will Freeman.) Will spends his days shooting pool, surfing porn and having his hair "carefully disheveled" at the salon.

The movie opens with Will, not the brightest bulb, watching the game show *Who Wants to Be a Millionaire*. The question is posed, "Who wrote the phrase 'No man is an island'? John Donne, John Milton, John F. Kennedy or Jon Bon Jovi."

"Jon Bon Jovi. Too easy!" Will answers to the television. "And, if I may say so, a complete load of bollocks."

From there he recounts his philosophy of life:

> In my opinion all men are islands. And what's more, now is the time to be one. This is an Island Age. A hundred years ago, for instance, you had to depend on other people. No one had TV or CDs or DVDs or videos or home espresso makers. In fact, they didn't have anything cool. Whereas now you see you can make yourself a little island paradise. With the right supplies and more importantly the right attitude you can be sundrenched, tropical, a magnet for young Swedish tourists. And I like to think, perhaps, I'm that kind of island.[1]

Soon Will is revealed to be shallow, pathetic and miserable. But through meeting a twelve-year-old boy and his severely depressed mother, Will is drawn out of himself and into a whole network of authentic relationships. The boy, Marcus, teaches Will that one person alone isn't enough. Even two are inadequate. You need plenty of backup.

By the end of the movie, enriched with many new friends, Will restates his philosophy of life: "Every man is an island, I stand by that. But, clearly, some men are part of island chains. Below the surface of the ocean, they're actually connected."

It's one of my (Greg's) all-time favorite movies. And as a person who has sometimes been accused of being emotionally distant, it chokes me up every time.

The Power of Two and More

Two are better than one,
because they have a good return for their labor:
If either of them falls down,
one can help the other up.

> *But pity anyone who falls*
> *and has no one to help them up.*
> *Also, if two lie down together, they will keep warm.*
> *But how can one keep warm alone?*
> *Though one may be overpowered,*
> *two can defend themselves.*
> *A cord of three strands is not quickly broken.*

ECCLESIASTES 4:9-12

Somehow amid the frustrations of life under the sun, Qoheleth comes to an island of respite: friendship. Your work may frustrate you, and your corporation may let you down, but cooperation never will. There are surefire benefits to community. It offers an entirely alternate vision of reality. Here's what we mean:

Over and over, Qoheleth asks, "What is the gain?" He uses a Hebrew word *yithron*, a business term that speaks of profit, earnings, capital gains. It's found nowhere else in the Bible, but it's used repeatedly in Ecclesiastes, revealing Solomon's overly commercial worldview. To him, everything is supposed to yield *yithron*.

That's a particular vision that many of us hold as well. It comes out in our very language. Just think about how often you hear business language used in nonbusiness contexts. "Let's get down to business." "Mind your own business." "Like nobody's business." And that's just a few usages of the word *business.* We're making *value propositions* all the time. We want *net* results in everything we do. *Bottom line*, we're always casting things in commercial terms.

But in Ecclesiastes 4, there's a different perspective. Friendship is described in noncommercial terms. Even the phrase "good return" or "good reward" isn't *yithron.* There's gain in friendship—help, warmth, security—but it doesn't have to be described in cash value terms.

And it's not about having just one source of backup but two. "A cord of three strands is not quickly broken" (Ecclesiastes 4:12b).

Although pastors like to cast that third party as God when using this text to talk about marriage, that's not the immediate meaning. Human triads have a potency that even duos lack. Any group of "three musketeers" experiences a multiplier effect that makes them more than the sum of their parts.

If Solomon wrote these words near the end of his life, they represent an impressive realization. Nowhere in Scripture do we see him having people who were able to confront him when he headed in the wrong direction. There are no indicators that in the prime of his life he had prophets or friends willing to inflict "faithful wounds" for his vanity or self-indulgence (Proverbs 27:6 NKJV).

What a contrast to his father. When David's opponents discouraged him, Jonathan strengthened his faith in God. When David committed adultery, Nathan made him face his guilt. When David proudly suggested taking a census of his fighting men, Joab rebuked his plan. Even though David failed at times, he was rebuked and returned, whereas Solomon went off the rails and stayed there.

The presence of friends certainly assisted me (Greg) in my midlife madness. When a particularly acute bout of "wandering heart disease" hit me, God gave me the good sense to tell a few trusted people about it; it's easier to confess your sins before you commit them. My friends offered support and prayers, and just knowing that they knew what I was going through helped immensely.

But separate prey from the pack, and you're *dead meat*.

Primal Loneliness

> *Again I looked and saw all the oppression that*
> *was taking place under the sun.*
>
> *I saw the tears of the oppressed—*
> *and they have no comforter;*

> *power was on the side of their oppressors—*
> *and they have no comforter.*

ECCLESIASTES 4:1

At my (Greg's) church, we highly value relationships, and our leaders have done a great job engaging people in small groups. We're well ahead of the national average for the percentage of our people who participate. One factoid heightening the urgency is that by age thirty-six, most people have made their last good friend. Especially men. Women tend to fare better, but by midlife many of us find friendships to be in dwindling supply. Right when we need them most.

Whether the oppression comes in the form of land seizure or loan sharking—like in many parts of the world—or just life stresses like in ours, we get by with help from our friends. Not a little. A lot.

And what a pitiful circumstance if we don't have them. The Teacher can only repeat the sad refrain, "And they have no comforter." Primal loneliness. Too many islands, too few island chains.

Human loneliness is primal because relationships are primal. They've existed in the Trinity for all eternity and were made central in creation. When God formed this wonderful, beautiful world, the only thing "not good" about it was the lack of a partner for Adam (Genesis 2:18). So God made a friend, and his creation was complete.

But one chapter later, in Genesis 3, it all falls apart. Adam and Eve eat the forbidden fruit, and the first consequence is alienation from each other and from God. Chronic loneliness ensues, touching all of us. Even with a spouse and friends, some dimensions of our souls are still isolated.

> Each heart knows its own bitterness,
> and no one else can share its joy. (Proverbs 14:10)

The problems of primal loneliness compound. It's twice as dangerous as obesity. Isolation impairs immune functions and boosts inflammation, both of which can lead to arthritis, type 2 diabetes and heart disease.[2]

This doesn't get fixed on social media. You can have hundreds of cyberfriends and upload your woes to them all. But research shows that posting your problems online makes you more likely to get discouraged. There's a self-fulfilling cycle on social media where people who gush about happy things get positive reinforcement, while sad people with sad posts get little feedback, causing them to isolate further.[3] If you need healing, you're unlikely to find it on Facebook.[4]

Fundamental Connection

In the movie *The Invention of Lying*, the screenwriters create a world where falsehood does not exist. Everyone and everything is hardwired for truth telling.

A sponsored message from Coke comes on the screen, saying, "Hi, I'm Bob. I'm the spokesperson for the Coca-Cola Company. I'm here today to ask you to continue buying Coke. Sure, it's a drink you've been drinking for years. It's basically just brown sugar water."[5]

A man walks into his office and is greeted by his assistant, who declares, "I realize more and more each day how overqualified I am for this position and how incompetent you are at yours."

A woman walks into a restaurant, and the hostess blurts out, "I'm threatened by you."

A man on the street holds up a sign saying, "I don't understand why I'm homeless and all of you are not."

As the plot progresses, some people decide to invent fiction—that is, lying, including falsehoods about a "Man in the Sky" who controls everything and promises great rewards in a good place you can go after you die. That's where the story becomes unpalatable for those of us who count God and his promises our most precious truths. But the premise of the movie is intriguing: What if everyone's default was set to truth telling? Would it cause us to divide and hide or to unite and connect?

Brené Brown believes people would connect. In a 2010 TED talk that has been viewed by over twenty million people, Brené describes her research as a social scientist and what it has taught her about vulnerability. After hearing countless stories and interviews, Brené was able to discern two basic categories of human beings: those who had a strong sense of belonging and those who had a prevailing sense of disconnection and primal longing. The difference came down to one fundamental thing: vulnerability.

All of us fear that if others really knew us, they wouldn't really love us. But people who connect with others face their fears and risk revealing themselves. They have the courage to be imperfect. They let go of their carefully crafted personas and put their real selves out there. Brené says,

> They fully embraced vulnerability. They believed that what made them vulnerable made them beautiful. They didn't talk about vulnerability being comfortable nor did they talk about it being really excruciating. They just talked about it being necessary. They talked about the willingness to say "I love you" first. The willingness to do something where there are no guarantees. The willingness to invest in a relationship that may or may not work out. They thought this was fundamental.[6]

She further describes these people with three Cs: courage to tell the story of who they are; compassion for themselves and others; and connection as a result of their authenticity. That's so "above the sun," isn't it? How do people find the courage to tell their real story unless they believe that love is at the center of it all? Unless they believe that their vulnerability and authenticity will be rewarded— if not by God, then at least by the universe?

I think the story of Jesus himself sets the pace. In the first chapter of the New Testament, Matthew 1, we read what many consider a boring and irrelevant list of names. It's Jesus' genealogy. The ancients reckoned their identity by their ancestry. Not that you weren't an individual person, but for the most part you were your family line. If you came from a noble, stable family, you were a noble, stable person. If your family was dysfunctional, so were you. You were the product of your lineage. Your genealogy doubled as your résumé and personal references.

So when we see that Jesus' line contains criminals and Gentiles and women of ill repute and a case of incest and some people who had been put under the divine ban—well, what does that say about him? Answer: that he's a real human being and that the Bible doesn't whitewash stories. And, wonderfully, that Jesus isn't ashamed to call us brothers and sisters. The one who makes us holy is part of our family (see Hebrews 2:10-13).

M. Scott Peck, author of *The Different Drum*, says this about authentic community: "When I am with a group of human beings committed to hanging in there through both the agony and the joy of community, I have a dim sense that I am participating in a phenomenon for which there is only one word. I almost hesitate to use it. The word is 'glory.'"[7]

Others-Focused Friendship

There's something radiant and weighty, not fleeting or empty—not *havel*—about a true Christian community. It's compelling to those inside and out. In fact, people will bang down the doors to be a part of it. From the earliest days of the church, the followers of Jesus were known for their friendship and love. Gracious hospitality was their best advertisement. Travelers were always welcome, whether the community knew them or not. Their generous spirit was so highly regarded that even the emperor noticed.

In the fourth century, the anti-Christian Roman Emperor Julian said, "Nothing has contributed to the progress of the superstition of the Christians as their charity to strangers. . . . They provide not only for their own poor, but for ours as well."[8] Julian saw such indiscriminate hospitality as a mark of the contentment, joy and inclusive nature of the Jesus movement. And he was right.

But it went further. During this volatile era, the empire was crumbling under the strain of outside raids and internal pestilence that took millions of lives. While the dead were piling up in the streets, the physicians left town, husbands left their wives and mothers left their dying children. The Bishop Dionysius remarked that the average person "pushed the sufferers away and fled from their dearest, throwing them into the roads before they were dead, and treated unburied corpses as dirt, hoping thereby to avert the spread and contagion of the fatal disease; but, do what they might, they found it difficult to escape."[9]

In contrast, the Christian community cared for its own sick and Rome's. Heedless of their own physical well-being, they took charge of the sick, attending to their needs in the name of Jesus. Some Christians died themselves, having contracted incurable illnesses from those they ministered to. But this ultimately led to the rapid growth of the church, as it went from 120 original followers to tens of millions within a few centuries.

Above the sun, relationships not only meet our needs, they also empower us to serve others. They give the whole group of us an irrepressible esprit de corps. That's precisely what we need in midlife, when circumstances hit us with any number of "plagues and epidemics." We need a band of friends to care for us and to be cared for by us. We need a group to minister to us and to mobilize us for ministry.

David Saint-Hilaire has served as a leader of Esperanza, a microfinance institution in Haiti. Like many around the world, he and his family offer humble but lavish displays of friendship.

One day my friend Kyle and I (Peter) were walking the dirt roads in flip-flops. You don't have to spend much time in Haiti's sweltering heat before you stink. But in our case, it wasn't just sweat that made us filthy; Kyle had stepped in some mud. So he asked for some water to wash up, but got more than he asked for. Instead of giving him water and a rag, David's sister dropped to her knees and washed his feet. He said he had never been so humbled.

Later we asked if we could use the bathroom. The Saint-Hilaires don't have indoor plumbing, just a pit latrine in the backyard. That was fine with us; we had roughed it before. But that wasn't satisfactory to them. So they turned a room in their house into a makeshift restroom. When we had to go, they held up a sheet for our privacy. If you needed toilet paper, a hand came around the corner, offering it.

As we sat down to a lunch they had spent the morning making, we experienced uncommon friendship. The meal of rice, beans, fish and fried plantains was served in old Communion trays. Plantains were stuffed into the slots where the cups typically rested. I don't think I've ever seen a more beautiful picture of Communion.

We had come to Haiti expecting to serve, but instead we were the recipients.

Tangible Expressions

The midlife crisis is often marked by a preoccupation with your life, your disappointments, your frustrations. But 40/40 vision is an outward-facing perspective. And it is an invitation to come truly alive. Use midlife time to practice self-revealing vulnerability and others-centered love. Be honest about your own dirty feet of clay, and wash the feet of others.

Determine over the next few months to make one new friend. At the same time, take care of those you already have. Don't let your relationships—the significant stuff of life—slip away through benign neglect. Even though I (Peter) am separated from many of my closest friends, I actually schedule time on my calendar to touch base with my closest core. Every Friday morning, I start the day with phone calls, a simple routine that has shielded both my friends and me from much midlife loneliness. Without intentional care, friendships, like all living things, begin to die.

Kristi Black, a blogger and mother of four, celebrated her fortieth birthday in an others-oriented way. During the week leading up to the milestone, she committed to doing forty random acts of kindness. She and her kids baked sugar cookies and gave them away. She paid the toll for the car behind her. She delivered donuts to the babysitter, bought coffee for a stranger, donated blood and let people go ahead of her in line.

"The big four-o. It's a pretty big milestone," Kristi wrote. "My birthday was not just memorable—it was the best birthday to date."[10]

What a powerful way to wrap up the first half of life and launch into the second!

10

(UN)CONTROLLABLE

How Do We Respond When
Circumstances Get the Best of Us?

The will of God is never exactly what you expect it to be.
It may seem to be much worse, but in the end, it's
going to be a lot better and a lot bigger.

ELISABETH ELLIOT

E leven months after getting his license, Joel drove like a pro. He
pushed the limits daily, speeding as a matter of course and sometimes even racing. One November Sunday, Joel was rushing from
church to a football field with a car full of guys. Cresting a small
hill, he hit the gas, going for that roller-coaster effect. About one
hundred yards ahead he saw an Amish buggy.

Central Pennsylvania is home to one of the world's largest
Amish community, and those of us living here have developed a
protocol for this sort of situation: you slow down, use a turn signal
and pass safely. Pretty much the same maneuver courteous drivers
use the world over. But some seventeen-year-olds aren't known
for manners—or braking.

"I'm going to blow by these guys," Joel announced to his passengers.

Stomping on the gas, he accelerated past seventy and steered into the passing lane. As he raced by, the nose of the horse flashed in front of him. The buggy was making a left turn.

"Instinct took over as I pounded the brake pedal with my foot. The brakes locked, and the car skidded forward, tires screaming. We smashed into the buggy, and I heard the pop of my windshield shattering to pieces," Joel recalls. "The buggy flew over the top of the car, and we rumbled to a stop in a field. My hands, still gripping the wheel, were streaming with blood, but only from shards of glass that grazed my knuckles. I still have a tiny scar between two knuckles on my left hand, a constant reminder that basically nothing happened to me."

After confirming the safety of everyone else in the car, Joel tried unsuccessfully to open his door. The collision had jammed it shut. Just then an Amish man came running up to the vehicle yelling, "Does anyone know CPR?"

Climbing out, Joel and his passengers were not prepared for what they saw. The Amish man was holding the crumpled pile of what looked like his mother. She was severely injured, convulsing and missing teeth. Two guys sprinted toward the nearest home in search of a phone. Eventually cars stopped, and the police and EMT crew came to the scene. Parents were informed, and families waited.

Eventually the news came back to Joel. Due to permanent brain damage, the woman would need life support to stay alive. The Amish don't believe in life support other than God, so Sarah died that night. The news worsened. Sarah wasn't the mother of the man; she was his wife, his newly wedded wife. Aaron and Sarah were on their honeymoon. They had been married five days. He was twenty-one; she was nineteen.

"It was and still is by far, the worst day of my life," Joel says. There were innumerable tears. Desperate prayers. Crushing guilt.

Joel was determined to go to the viewing but was so nervous

beforehand that he felt physical pain. "Would they come pouring out of the house with shotguns?" That's what he imagined.

Unsure of the viewing's location, Joel's family mistakenly drove to Aaron's home. There they were immediately surrounded by Aaron's relatives, who hugged them and expressed forgiveness. Aaron's father needed a lift to the viewing, so he rode with Joel's family, guiding the way. While reserved, he too expressed forgiveness.

When they arrived at Sarah's home, buggies filled the property. *How do I face all these people?* Joel got out of the car and walked into the dimly lit house. Sarah's family had heard Joel was coming and met him in the front room. The woman's parents, Melvin and Barbara Stoltzfus, put their arms around him and uttered the most incredible words he had ever heard: "We forgive you."

As if verbal forgiveness were not enough, they invited Joel's family for dinner sometime in the coming weeks. Then someone led Joel to a back room, where Aaron stood beside Sarah's open casket. Aaron went to Joel with open arms. The two young men hugged, the freedom of forgiveness being granted in the embrace.

In the ensuing months, the Stoltzfus family never once attempted to pass blame or exact revenge. On the contrary, they intentionally got to know Joel and his family, exchanging stories and comparing their two cultures. As the Amish have become renowned for doing, they opened their heart to the other.

"I still have a pile of at least fifty cards that I received from various Amish people across the county," Joel recalls. "They were constantly encouraging and pointing me to God. Since that time, I've never had trouble forgiving other people. It flows out as naturally as my heart beats, without me having a say in the matter."

But there were still crimes committed and legal proceedings to endure. "My trial and punishment served as another opportunity for the Amish family to demonstrate their forgiveness. They wrote letters to the judge, begging for my pardon, asking that I be acquitted on all counts." Joel was not acquitted but charged with vehicular homicide. Spared a jail sentence due to his age, he got off with a revoked license, probation and community service.

Five years later, the Stoltzfus family joyfully attended Joel's wedding, bearing gifts. And three years after that, when Joel and his wife became missionaries, their Amish friends supported them.

Extreme forgiveness—it may be the greatest contribution of the Amish community to the wider world. Immediately after the Nickel Mines shooting in 2006, similar grace was extended in a way the watching world just couldn't comprehend. The day after burying their daughters, the parents attended the shooter's funeral, hugging his widow and his family.[1]

We scratch our heads and wonder, *How do they do that?* And in the darker recesses of our hearts we ask, *Should they?* It's not fair, and life is supposed to be fair.

Inevitable Injustice

If you see the poor oppressed in a district, and justice and rights denied, do not be surprised at such things; for one official is eyed by a higher one, and over them both are others higher still. The increase from the land is taken by all; the king himself profits from the fields.

ECCLESIASTES 5:8-9

It's a thirty-two-hour ordeal to get to the small town of Kisangani in the Democratic Republic of Congo. It's even more difficult to leave. A shady official in customs was harassing us, searching for any excuse for a bribe. Corruption is thick among government officials in a kleptocracy.

Time was on his side, and the more he delayed, the more he knew we'd grow agitated. Finally he let us pass, but pointed across the hall to another checkpoint, where we would have to get cleared by the

Ministry of Health before boarding our plane.

As we walked across the hall, we watched this same official put on a white lab coat and walk into his other office. I wasn't sure whether to laugh or cry. Trying to look "medical," he began the negotiations again.

In places of poverty, it's easy to feel like the world is spinning out of control. There is turmoil on every level and deep suffering in every system. In Haiti, I once watched mothers baking a mixture of dirt and flour so their children would have enough to eat. These families did not deserve this; it was simply the result of where they lived. Not far away, people had plenty.

Even Qoheleth can make only cynical sense of it. He says that each layer of injustice is superimposed on another. Little officials are overseen by medium officials who are overseen by large officials until you get to the king. And that's where the gain is. In a rare use of the word *gain*, Qoheleth (who usually says there is no gain) says, "But this is gain for a land in every way: a king committed to cultivated fields" (ESV).

One translator replaces *official* in Ecclesiastes 5:8 with *arrogant one*, rendering the verse, "An arrogant one is above an arrogant one, and arrogant ones have watched over them all."[2] So at the end of the day, you have kings—kings interested in fields, because they tax every last one of them.

Why be surprised? says the Teacher. It's a cruel world. The strong eat the weak. Injustice suffuses the system.

Casual Calamity

> *I have seen something else under the sun:*
>
> > *The race is not to the swift*
> > *or the battle to the strong,*

> *nor does food come to the wise*
> *or wealth to the brilliant*
> *or favor to the learned;*
> *but time and chance happen to them all.*

Moreover, no one knows when their hour will come:

> *As fish are caught in a cruel net,*
> *or birds are taken in a snare,*
> *so people are trapped by evil times*
> *that fall unexpectedly upon them.*

ECCLESIASTES 9:11-12

I (Greg) once went on a website that morbidly offered a personal death clock. You punched in your date of birth and some health info, and then declared your basic outlook on life: optimistic, pessimistic or sadistic. Being a reasonably hopeful person I chose "Optimistic" and punched Enter.

December 25, 2050. That's when I'll die. (Note to self: open your presents on Christmas Eve in 2050.) I'll be eighty-seven. Thankfully I still have over a billion seconds left.

But of course that assumes my good fortunes hold for another three and a half decades. They may not. In fact, it might be odd if they did, because as Qoheleth observes, the forces of time, chance and unexpected evil stalk us all.

A child suffers a stroke and becomes confined to a chair, nonverbal.

A young woman in her twenties develops brain cancer.

An expert scuba diver has a mild heart attack that he would have survived anywhere else except underwater.

An astute businessman who formerly saw everything he touched turn to gold, suddenly can't buy a break. Now every venture turns to lead.

These aren't hypotheticals. They are actual events that have happened to people in my church. And what's frightening is that they seem so random.

Jerry Sittser is a professor of religion at Whitworth College in Spokane, Washington. He tells the story of an evening when his wife, Lynda, returned from choir practice at 10:00 p.m. The two drank hot chocolate together, then crawled into bed, talking and laughing until 12:30 in the morning. Just before saying good night, Lynda said, "Jerry, I can't imagine life being any better than it is right now. It is so wonderful to me. I am overcome by the goodness of God."[3] Less than twenty-four hours later, Jerry's wife and mother and daughter were gone, killed by a drunk driver.

In a chapter titled "The Terror of Randomness," Sittser reflects:

> One of the worst aspects of my experience of loss has been this sense of sheer randomness. The event was completely outside my control—an "accident" as we say. The threat of *anomie*, as Peter Berger has called this disorderliness, was and still is almost unbearable to me. . . . I looked with cynicism on the absurdity of life. Maybe, I thought, there really is no God and no meaning to life. I resigned myself to misery and death, thereby yielding to its inexorability.[4]

Life's setbacks, whether truly tragic or just painfully inconvenient, may be hardest to overcome in midlife. When we're young, we have the time and energy to bounce back. When we're old, we have fewer expectations and a bigger bank of wisdom and experience to draw upon. But when that snare springs in the middle of life, right when we thought we had it all figured out, we wonder if we can escape and recover.

The Illusion of Control

I have a wealthy friend who once confided that the problem with most rich people is they think they're experts at everything. They seem to think they can secure their own lives and solve the world's problems, simply because they've made it in a certain field. And with all the securities money can buy—financial and otherwise—they create an aura of invincibility.

Many of the rest of us attempt to follow suit. To create and maintain a sense of safety and control, we move from city to suburb to exurb. We install locks, alarms and surveillance cameras. We wear helmets, goggles and seat belts. We take everything from karate to multivitamins. We cocoon ourselves in everything from barbed wire to sunscreen.

Ann Patchett once wrote, "Staving off our own death is one of our favorite national pastimes. Whether it's exercise, checking our cholesterol or having a mammogram, we are always hedging against mortality. Find out what the profile is, and identify the ways in which you do not fit it."[5]

But inevitably something happens to remind us that we're neither as smart nor as competent as we think. We fail. We suffer loss. Or the task of parenting teenagers brings us to our knees. The illusion of omnicompetence is shattered. Heck, half the time we can't even control our own emotions. And then it hits us: this sorry state of affairs would be normal if we ran the world. Were it not for countless days of grace, we'd be this skittish all the time.

Our Times Are in Your Hands

> *There is a time for everything,*
> *and a season for every activity under the heavens:*
>
> *a time to be born and a time to die,*
> *a time to plant and a time to uproot,*
> *a time to kill and a time to heal,*

> *a time to tear down and a time to build,*
> *a time to weep and a time to laugh,*
> *a time to mourn and a time to dance,*
> *a time to scatter stones and a time to gather them,*
> *a time to embrace and a time to refrain from embracing,*
> *a time to search and a time to give up,*
> *a time to keep and a time to throw away,*
> *a time to tear and a time to mend,*
> *a time to be silent and a time to speak,*
> *a time to love and a time to hate,*
> *a time for war and a time for peace. . . .*
> *He has made everything beautiful in its time.*

ECCLESIASTES 3:1-8, 11

This is probably one of the ten best poems of all time. Certainly one of the most enduring. It's so beautifully rhythmic in its presentation of the warp and woof of life: joy and sorrow, sickness and healing, war and peace, birth and death. There's no randomness here, just divine order. Yes, our days oscillate between the good and the bad, but with a harmonic pattern.

Look at your life. Can you see the blessings running lengthwise through it, from start to finish? Who, recognizing the sheer goodness of God's creation and provision, can't see it? David said in Psalm 23, "Surely goodness and love will follow me all the days of my life." And we have to affirm, "Mine too."

But then pain interlaces itself in our experience, cutting across the grain of God's longitudinal blessings. That's the meaning of the idiom "warp and woof," by the way: threads running lengthwise and crosswise in a fabric.

This brings us to the old illustration of a medieval tapestry, with a beautiful picture on one side and a lot of loose ends on the other. God is weaving all the joys and troubles of life into a whole cloth with a coherent picture. I like Qoheleth's use of the present perfect tense in "He has made everything beautiful in its time." You might not see it, but that doesn't mean it's not already accomplished in the counsels of God. It's kind of like Paul's New Testament statement that "God has raised us up with Christ and seated us with him in the heavenly realms" (Ephesians 2:6). It hasn't happened with full literalness yet, but Christ's accomplishment is so full and irrevocable that we might as well talk about it being done already.

Way back in the book of Genesis, we read the story of Jacob and Joseph. Jacob is the third great patriarch of Israel. It's always "Abraham, Isaac and Jacob." In fact, Jacob was the patriarch that God renamed Israel, with his twelve boys becoming the twelve tribes. But the path to that beautiful result was anything but smooth.

Joseph was sold by his jealous brothers into slavery, then passed off to his father as dead. Years later, when he rose to be prince of Egypt, the other sons of Jacob appeared before him, looking to buy food. A series of intrigues ensued. Brother Simeon was taken hostage, and the prince of Egypt demanded that Benjamin appear before him too. Benjamin, of course, had not made the trip, being his father's new favorite.

At that point, Jacob cried out, "You have deprived me of my children. Joseph is no more and Simeon is no more, and now you want to take Benjamin. Everything is against me!" (Genesis 42:36).

That's the way it looks on the back side of the tapestry, under the sun. But from a God's-eye view, the exact opposite is true. Everything isn't against Jacob; everything is for him. God is bringing about the rescue of the people, the reconciliation of the family, the redemption of the whole world! But all in due time.

More than a decade on from the loss of three family members, Sittser marveled at God's sovereign genius.

Obviously the loss my children and I suffered was irreversible. As I have already written, I will never have Lynda, Diana Jane, or my mother back again. The goodness they contributed to my life and the goodness we shared together are gone forever. Yet I can say without a moment's hesitation that my life has been very good since the accident occurred, though not as I had planned or imagined. It is almost a surprise to me, as if learning I had just inherited a million dollars from some cranky uncle whom I had never liked. I find it hard to fathom or explain. I can only say that it is grace, pure grace. How could so much good come out of something that was so unequivocally bad?[6]

Midlife calls us to muster enough faith to believe not only that "this too shall pass," but also that this too shall pass into the category of The Beautiful. God will make it so in its time.

Three Losses of Control

There are at least three kinds of control losses that might befall us, and all three have their redemptive upside—the beautiful side of the tapestry.

1. When things happen to us. In the middle of dinner, Emily Johnson began slurring her words. Immediately concerned, they skipped the rest of the meal, and her husband, Stephen, rushed her to the hospital. Within two hours, Emily had lost consciousness from a brain bleed. Days later, she was gone.

For decades, Stephen and Emily had planned for retirement. They had worked hard and tithed faithfully, all the while imagining a happy, secure future. But in a moment, Stephen's life changed. Having worked so hard to build a future, he realized he had missed too much of the present. And now the future he had imagined was no more.

So with renewed passion for his faith and family, Stephen turned his focus toward helping single moms escape poverty. By providing job preparedness and skills training, along with practical things like clothing for interviews, he is using the rest of his life to serve others.

Even his nest egg is being used to help others build nests. Tragedy provided the raw material for Stephen to make a difference while enacting a different future.

2. *When things happen through us.* At times, we do things that cause our own lives to spin out of control. These cut deep, because we not only disappoint others but also become ashamed of ourselves.

Robert and Lynn are some of the most generous and wise people you would ever hope to meet. Throughout their lives, they have sought to love the Lord with all their hearts. Along with their four children, all of whom follow Jesus too, the family enjoys an unusual closeness.

But one evening a few years ago, Lynn was on the family computer when she came upon an unfamiliar email account. She opened it and found inappropriate exchanges between Robert and one of her friends. Soon the truth came out: the two were engaged in an emotional affair.

The next day, a devastated Lynn confided in her adult daughter, Noelle. "I still remember what I was doing, changing the sheets on my bed, when I got the call letting me know what happened," Noelle relates. "I listened quietly, tried not to ask too many questions, hung up—and then began sobbing uncontrollably. Our greatest vulnerabilities as a family were realized. It was a dark time on a relational as well as spiritual level."

In midlife, the stakes are high. A brief indiscretion can threaten everything we've spent years building: our marriages, our professions, our families, even our faith. But the turning point in this story was not Robert's infidelity. It was his humble response to the confrontation. He confessed his sin, sought forgiveness and relinquished control to his wife and others as he sought counseling to grapple with the root of the problem. Robert and Lynn worked to repair their relationship, and God turned a former weakness into a true strength, both for them and for others.

As a result of seeing her parents struggle and prevail, Noelle says that she and her husband were encouraged as they navigated significant issues in their very first year of marriage. "All my life, I'd been grateful for the strength of my parents' marriage," she says. "But more recently I've grown grateful for their willingness to talk with me about the frailty in their marriage. I've seen the kingdom of heaven break in through God's redemption of both our marriages."

When life spins out of control because of our poor choices, the quickest way to renew equilibrium and restore blessing is surrender. That is one decision within our control—the decision to relinquish control. And by exercising that choice, we welcome God's redemption into our lives. (As someone once said, "Whatever the issue is, the issue is control.")

3. *When things happen for us.* We opened this chapter with a story of scandalous grace: the story of Joel and the grace he received after killing a young woman. It wasn't fair. And some of us might have such a strong attachment to justice that we think it was wrong. How could Aaron and his Amish community forgive Joel so freely? How could they plead to the court to drop all charges and let him go? Because Jesus suffered the ultimate injustice. He was the only person who ever deserved full acquittal from every possible charge. But instead of being set free, he suffered the most excruciating death. Crucifixion. (*Crucifixion* and *excruciating* share the same root.)

Jesus not only lacked all sin, he also possessed all merit. He was the glorious and eternal Son of God. The fact that he healed the sick, cleansed the leprous, fed the hungry and raised the dead was only superficial evidence of his excellence and perfection. But Jesus did all this and then laid down his life, suffering a fate that was a cosmic outrage. Yet in that human injustice, divine justice was served. Sin was atoned for so that forgiveness could be extended to all.

This was a kind of gain that even wise Qoheleth, living when and where he did, couldn't conceive. He saw random evils overtaking unsuspecting people. He saw rampant injustice running up through lower magistrates to the throne of the king. But what he couldn't see was divine providence and redemptive justice running up through the evil decisions of magistrates, of governors, of kings— all the way to the throne of heaven—until God said, "There, that does it. That completes the picture. I have made even the ultimate injustice beautiful in its time."

(DE)HUMANIZING

How Do You Maintain an Identity
Apart from Your Job?

Success is the world's criterion of merit; fidelity is God's.

CHARLES S. ROBINSON

Waking at 2 a.m., I (Peter) heard Laurel rush to the restroom. Groggily, I entered the bathroom to rub her back while she bent over the toilet. "Can I get you anything?" I tenderly asked. Hearing no response, I continued, "Cold towel? Pepto?"

"Please leave," was her sole response. No emotion in her voice. Just one very clear request.

Back in bed, I thought about my upcoming trip. In just a few hours, I was supposed to leave for California. But Laurel was sick, and she was pregnant. Listening to the toilet flush, I reached for my phone and started tapping out an email to cancel my trip.

But then, if I stay home, what can I really do? I stopped tapping. The evening before, I'd contacted someone to help with the kids. Our friends would respond with chicken soup. And Laurel had a doctor's appointment the next day, where she'd be given antibiotics or whatever she needed. Mentally running through my checklist of helpful actions, I concluded there was nothing more I could do. And clearly Laurel didn't want my help anyway. Besides, I had to go on the trip. It was a short and important meeting with individuals who could help us significantly expand HOPE's ministry.

Finishing my mental gymnastics, I nailed the dismount, arched my back and extended my arms. Lover at home; killer at work. *Let's do this thing.* I deleted the email, rolled over and fell back asleep.

When the alarm went off a few hours later, I saw that Laurel was sleeping soundly. Confirmation. Getting up, I performed my well-rehearsed routine like a ninja: silently showering, shaving and making coffee in less than twenty minutes. I skipped the normal kiss goodbye—*don't want to wake her*—and slipped out of the house.

In the car, I reassured myself. "I'll be back soon," I said out loud.

Opening the TED Talks app on my phone, I began listening to sociologist Dan Buettner on how to live to one hundred. Drawing from a study of regions where a high percentage of people enjoy prolonged lifespans, Buettner shared insights on how to live a full life. Oddly none of the wisdom involved choosing a business trip over caring for a sick spouse. That's when it hit me. *Live to be a hundred? I might not make it to next week.*

Back home, Laurel felt abandoned after waking up to find me gone. "If you prioritized and cared for me," she later said, "there is no way you would have left when I was sick, pregnant *and* it was snowing." Her words were succinct and sobering. There was simply no arguing who was right.

Choosing to go on the trip indicated a bigger problem: I had a faulty understanding of my calling and too much of my identity bound up in work. When I left for the airport that morning, I was following a pattern deeply engrained through years of practice. When challenges arose in my family, I would try to help, but I never seemed to do so in exactly the right way or at the right time. So I fled to work, where I was better at solving problems, where people recognized my expertise and where I could be successful. *Success at work came far easier than success at home.*

Over time, I convinced myself that leaving was good for both Laurel and for me. I was never a very good multitasker, and traveling allowed me to put the challenges of home out of my mind. So by the time midlife arrived, work had a firm, two-fisted hold on my heart. Leaving Laurel when she was sick sent a clear message—*I value work over you.* And that took quite some time to repair.

What is it about work that makes it so sovereign and irresistible? It drives us, controls us and, if we let it, transforms us into people we never thought we'd be.

Physical Reminders

Beyond the relational toll, an obsessive view of work eventually causes our bodies to rebel. Just ask my friend Ghena.

When the financial crisis hit in 2008, it didn't just strike Wall Street investors. It impacted every level of the global economy. In Moldova, a microfinance institution called Invest-Credit saw a rapidly increasing amount of its portfolio at risk, as families were slower to repay their loans. This raised concerns from donors and investors, who questioned the long-term viability of the program.

Ghena Russu, the executive director, worked tirelessly with his staff to resolve the problem. They spent more time visiting clients, scrutinizing all aspects of their enterprise and fastidiously measuring improvements. Nothing moved the needle. In fact, the more they worked, the more their problems grew.

As the leader of the organization, Ghena took the challenges personally. After working for weeks without a day off, he physically reacted to the stress. Unable to sleep or eat solid foods, he lost over twenty-five pounds in a month. Plagued by headaches, he sometimes had to pull his car off the road until they passed. Eventually he spent four weeks in the hospital while the doctors tried to diagnose his illness.

In the end it was simple: too much work, too little rest. When pushed too hard, our bodies whisper, "Please stop." If ignored, they raise their voices. Finally, like a pressure cooker with no relief valve, they explode. Overwork is eventually unworkable.

The Japanese have a word for it: *karōshi*, "death from overwork," sudden death from too much overtime. Many of us in midlife come dangerously close to experiencing it.

The Proverbial Ladder Against the Wrong Wall

So I hated life, because the work that is done under the sun was grievous to me. All of it is meaningless, a chasing after the wind. I hated all the things I had toiled for under the sun.

Up until the midpoint of his life, Solomon had boundless energy and ambition. He knew unrivaled success in his work. At its apex, his empire reached all the way from the Mediterranean Sea to the Euphrates River, in modern Iraq. Solomon had control of the two primary trade routes, the Via Maris by the sea and the King's Highway farther inland. Anyone traveling those roads to do business had to pay tolls. Solomon had a treaty with the Phoenicians who owned the seaports, but his status made him the majority partner. He contracted with the Phoenicians to build ships and send out expeditions. Historians tell us these ships went out on three-year expeditions around the known world to bring its treasures to Israel.

Solomon's building projects were legendary. He constructed the temple in Jerusalem, a magnificent structure overlaid with cedar and gold; it took seven years to complete. But his own palace may have been even more impressive, taking almost twice as long to build.

However, it wasn't just a few capital projects in Jerusalem that Solomon undertook. He built entire cities, erected military outposts, dug reservoirs and planted groves of trees. The word for these gardens was *paredes*, from which we get *paradise*. Ruins of his cisterns still exist, over a football field in area and thirty feet deep, capable of containing millions of gallons of water in that semiarid region. Solomon masterminded it all.

He had flocks and herds and four thousand stables for his horses (2 Chronicles 9:25). A patron of the arts, Solomon himself penned more than a thousand songs. He also hired musicians and singers to perform for him.

All that to say, if anybody was going to find satisfaction in his work, it was going to be Solomon. Yet, in the end, he found it *grievous.* It made him *hate* life.

What a mirror to our own lives. What a commentary on our own careers.

And Then What?

I hated all the things I had toiled for under the sun, because I must leave them to the one who comes after me. And who knows whether that person will be wise or foolish? Yet they will have control over all the fruit of my toil into which I have poured my effort and skill under the sun. This too is meaningless. So my heart began to despair over all my toilsome labor under the sun. For a person may labor with wisdom, knowledge and skill, and then they must leave all they own to another who has not toiled for it. This too is meaningless and a great misfortune.

ECCLESIASTES 2:18-21

Part of the problem with work is the knowledge that we'll leave what we've built to someone else, and we'll have no control over what happens next. What we spend decades building could be dismantled in days.

In almost every sphere, someone will take over where I leave off. They'll live in my house, occupy my office and do my job. And what if they don't bring the same passion? Or worse, what if they have an entirely different vision?

We might hand the ball to our kids, but next-generation family businesses often don't do well. Likewise, inheritances have a terrible track record of bettering the lives of their recipients. Trust-fund babies rarely have happy stories.

Maybe that's why Solomon looked at his potential heirs and concluded they were fools. It's easy to project onto others what we loathe in ourselves. We wonder why we put our heart and soul into our careers, and then we wonder how our kids will be any different. And yet it's not as simple as telling our kids not to work so hard. Many of us look at the next generation rising and wonder where a proper work ethic went.

So midlife is a time to think soberly about both what motivates us and what will motivate our children. We need to navigate deftly between making too much of our careers and helping our children to make enough of theirs. Our work is so *havel*, so maddeningly temporary.

The Wonders of Widget Making

A person can do nothing better than to eat and drink and find satisfaction in their own toil. This too, I see, is from the hand of God, for without him, who can eat or find enjoyment? To the person who pleases him, God gives wisdom, knowledge and happiness, but to the sinner he gives the task of gathering and storing up wealth to hand it over to the one who pleases God. This too is meaningless, a chasing after the wind.

ECCLESIASTES 2:24-26

Qoheleth commends a kind of existentialism in which all individuals find meaning in "their own toil." If it puts food on the table in a way that honors and pleases God, that is enough. In fact, anything else may be an overreach—an ambition to build a tower to the sky and make a name for oneself, which God has never viewed kindly.

In the New Testament, James echoes Qoheleth when he writes,

> Now listen, you who say, "Today or tomorrow we will go to this or that city, spend a year there, carry on business and make money." Why, you do not even know what will happen tomorrow. What is your life? You are a mist that appears for a little while and then vanishes. Instead, you ought to say, "If it is the Lord's will, we will live and do this or that." As it is, you boast in your arrogant schemes. All such boasting is evil. (James 4:13-16)

Similarly Paul commends modest hard work:

> But godliness with contentment is great gain. For we brought nothing into the world, and we can take nothing out of it. But if we have food and clothing, we will be content with that. Those who want to get rich fall into temptation and a trap and into many foolish and harmful desires that plunge people into ruin and destruction. For the love of money is a root of all kinds of evil. Some people, eager for money, have wandered from the faith and pierced themselves with many griefs. (1 Timothy 6:6-10)

Not that we merely work for food. Our vocations are callings from God, based on our gifts, passions, experiences and opportunities. Our work is purposeful. Have you heard the old tale of the construction crew queried by a passerby?

"What are you doing?" a passerby asks the first worker.

"Stacking bricks," he says flatly.

"And how about you?" a second worker is asked. "What are you doing?"

"Mixing cement," he grunts.

Looking to the third worker, the passerby inquires, "And what are you doing?"

"I'm building a cathedral!" comes the enthusiastic reply.

It's easy to get ground down by the day-to-day tasks of mixing cement and stacking bricks. In the Middle Ages, thousands of "working stiffs" did that their entire lives, erecting places of worship that would not be completed in their lifetime; they would not even get to see their work come to fruition. Still, many worked with devout hearts and eyes of faith, and many are receiving their eternal reward. So, "whatever you do, work at it with all your heart, as working for the Lord, not for human masters, since you know that you will receive an inheritance from the Lord as a reward. It is the Lord Christ you are serving" (Colossians 3:23-24).

I (Greg) saw a great example of this in my own living room recently. At the end of every membership class at our church, my wife and I host a dinner in our home. It's a chance to interact with the many new people joining our mission. After everyone has had a couple of passes through the buffet line, we always play the same get-to-know-you game. It's like show-and-tell for big people. Everyone brings an object that says something about his or her life. We've had people introduce themselves via sports equipment, handcrafts, rocks, plants, coins, photos, trophies—you name it. One time a guy brought a Maasai warrior spear because he had grown up on the mission field. Another brought a surfboard because he'd never grown up.

But one of my favorite objects was a little metal widget, just a little fastener that fit in the palm of a hand. Showing it to the group, Walt said, "This little fastener has put a roof over our heads, food on the table, three kids through college and two daughters into marriage. I have a little company that makes these things. It doesn't look like much, but it's made a life for me and my family."

Beautiful. The man isn't a brain surgeon or rocket scientist. None of his end users know his name or celebrate his accomplishments. His company may or may not endure beyond his lifetime. But his children have been raised, educated and successfully launched. His family has had a life. And many people have purchased products that work well and don't fall apart, because Walt saw to it.

That's meaningful, worthwhile, God-honoring work.

(Un)Stuck Under the Sun

But maybe just providing for your family isn't doing it for you anymore. Many people make midcourse career changes. In fact, the person who stays in one field for an entire working life is no longer the rule but the exception. Midlife rumblings can spur us to evaluate, to reprioritize and to break free if we feel trapped in a dead-end career.

Do you feel trapped? Why?

The financial trap. Many people become addicted to a lifestyle that requires big money to maintain. A while back, I (Peter) interviewed a potential employee at HOPE. Early on, he seemed like the ideal fit for the role. He even let us know that he and his family were willing to make sacrifices to join a nonprofit. "I'm able to dramatically decrease my compensation," he stated. My curiosity was piqued. And then he added, "But we still need just over $200,000 in salary." I picked up my jaw from the floor and quickly ended the conversation.

The fear trap. Many of us refuse to make a change because we can't stop wondering, *What if it doesn't work out?* We start to believe that a career is a freeway with a thousand exits and only one entrance. If we get off to try something new and it doesn't work out, will we ever find our way back?

The prestige trap. Sometimes our need for prestige keeps us stuck. We allow ourselves to be defined by our work or a particular role. Our identity becomes so tightly enmeshed with a title that giving it up would mean losing part of ourselves.

The retirement trap. The retirement trap is particularly subtle and perilous. The Bible extols the virtue of saving. Socking it away for retirement seems like the responsible thing to do. In old age, nobody wants to be a burden to her children or a ward of the state. But then again, Jesus said, "Do not store up for yourselves treasures on earth" (Matthew 6:19). Oversaving becomes a thin mask for an idolatrous desire to secure our own lives. We look forward to rest in retirement instead of eternal rest in God's kingdom. We may even think that once we stop working, we'll really start living.

Phil had counted down the days to retirement, when he would be free at last, free at last, thank God Almighty, free at last. He had saved judiciously, planned thoroughly. Walking out the door of his office for the last time with a celebratory piece of cake, he entered a new stage, with time on his hands.

But the reality of retirement didn't match the advertisements. After moving to Arizona and spending a couple of years playing golf and tennis, Phil felt trapped. It just wasn't the life of bliss he had dreamed of. "I *had* to play golf every afternoon," he said. "And I slowly started feeling like I did when I *had* to go to work every day. It sounds terrible, but what was once an enjoyable hobby became miserable." *This too is meaningless.*

Research has shown that traditional retirement is actually bad for your health. One study of 5,422 people showed a 40 percent increase in heart attack and stroke among retirees as compared to their peers who kept working.[1] The risk of developing clinical depression in the year after retirement is also 40 percent.[2]

In *A Resilient Life*, author Gordon MacDonald explained his views on this subject:

> A long time ago I dropped the word *retirement* out of my vo-
> cabulary. I don't believe in it. In the aging process, slowing up
> in tandem with one's diminishing strength might be a ne-

cessity. But retirement suggests, at least to me, a transition from activity to inactivity, from giving to taking. Where in the Scriptures does one find permission to do that? We are called, *at all times of our lives,* to be generous with our time.[3]

The What-For of Work

We humans used to live in a lush paradise not unlike Solomon's gardens. But life wasn't just a Sunday stroll. Even before sin sullied things, causing Adam to eke out a living "by the sweat of his brow," there was work. The first humans were placed in the Garden for the specific purpose of working and tending it (see Genesis 2:15).

Work was a good thing, a God thing. Through *work,* God created the world in the first place. He designed the planet to require our custodianship. Work is central to our existence and part of our *imago Dei,* part of our imaging of God. So all human labor was to be done in the light of God's model and mandate.

It was also to be done in the context of God's supply. In the Garden, life didn't depend on work; it depended on God. He had already provided for life in all he made, which had within it generative powers to bring forth more. As a result, Adam and Eve could exert themselves, but they had no need to exhaust themselves. They could enjoy work without having either their identities or their destinies bound up in it.

"Okay," you say, "but this isn't Eden."

No, it's not. We live outside the Garden and on the wrong side of the fall. But we also live on the right side of the cross and resurrection, which is where God did his heaviest lifting. Redemption is what we call *the work* of Christ.

Through that work, God secures our eternal well-being and underscores his ability to meet our temporal needs as well. He frees us to work for the flourishing of all people and of the planet he made. We

oo

get to seek first his kingdom—beyond the sun—with the promise of his supply for our daily needs. "And all these things will be given to you as well," Jesus said (Matthew 6:33). Or as Paul put it, life does not depend on human will or exertion, but on God's mercy (Romans 9:16).

So, as easy as it is to be sucked too deeply into *a job*, we must remember that we were made for *meaningful work*. Work is good for our physical, psychological and emotional well-being—not to mention the world it serves. The happiest people never retire; they just redirect their energies into new areas of service.

Recognizing he was created for work, Phil ended his retirement. He stopped golfing every afternoon and started writing books and blogs. He became an active investor in companies that are making a difference. And he is much more engaged, healthy and happy.

Most of us will reach that day when others are no longer willing to pay us. Consider it not retirement but redeployment. You might not be useful to your company anymore, but you're useful to God always. And it's not too early to start musing over what that future season might look like for you.

Transitioning Those Paid and Unpaid

Bob Buford had a successful cable television company when he came to the midpoint of his life. As he navigated questions common to those in their forties, he realized he'd spent the first half of his life working for success, not significance. Determined to make a change—and a difference—Bob founded the Halftime Institute, a nonprofit organization that coaches people into significance in the latter half of their lives. It has impacted thousands, including Dave Wasik, HOPE's vice president of operations.

After climbing the corporate ladder at a successful company for eighteen years, Dave's wife, Jen, gave him a Bible that mapped out reading the entire book in a year. For the first time in his life, Dave read the Word intensively. "If the Bible is true, then it demands my life, my soul, my all," he concluded. Although he had always called himself a Christian, he realized he'd given his best to his employer and his leftovers to God. "I had a sudden recalibration on what matters and knew it was time for me to step out."

At age forty and at the top of his career, Dave took a leave of absence to explore what might come next. "I didn't know what I was going to do," he said. "For a few days, I was fearful and disillusioned."

But after participating in Halftime Institute's career consulting, Dave joined HOPE International and is using his talents to fight global poverty. "The idea of working in the difficult places where we have programs seemed like an adventure, not something scary or inconvenient," he said. "It was a leap of faith in the purest sense."

Whether you've spent your career running a company or running a house full of kids, your forties are a time to look forward vocationally. Having just dropped off her youngest child at college, Brianna said, "I feel like I was just fired from the best job I could ever have." Some parents face this new stage with fist pumps, others with fear. For a mom who has poured herself into her children, midlife can be as disorienting as any job loss. With dependents in the rearview mirror and tears clouding your eyes, it can be hard to see your way forward.

When Nancy Gast still had three very young children, she anticipated the day they would be independent, and she made preparations. When her kids started elementary school, Nancy went back to graduate school to become a licensed occupational therapist. Despite the challenge of schooling herself while raising kids, her vision was crystal clear. And her second career proved to be an ideal combination of reasonable pay, workable hours and the engaging mission of helping patients recover from traumatic illnesses and accidents.

Back to Ghena—and Reality

Sometimes a change in our work reorients us to others. And sometimes it reorients us to ourselves. With little to do but think, my friend Ghena reacquainted himself with his real priorities. The forced sabbatical brought on by his breakdown gave him time to dialogue with God about foundational work questions. *Is my identity defined by this role? Do the numbers at work measure my value as a person? Why am I literally killing myself like this?*

"Staring at the hospital ceiling, I eventually came to my senses like a prodigal son," Ghena said. And he came home to the realization that his identity was not in what he did but whose he was. He was the son of a loving heavenly Father; he was a younger brother to Jesus. Work was a calling and a gift, but not the foundation of his life.

And Ghena's health began to improve—in every department. Having learned some hard-won lessons, he created boundaries to protect himself from stress. He reduced his hours, forced himself to take days off and exercised more frequently. And he publicly acknowledged his mistakes, asking the Invest-Credit staff to forgive him for linking his worth to his work—which in his case is inextricably linked to the state of the global economy. Not exactly something he can control.

A Keystone Habit

In his book *The Power of Habit*, Charles Duhigg describes certain practices that trigger a series of healthy behaviors. He calls them "keystone habits." For example, I (Greg) have found that when my diet goes south, if I drink a glass of water before meals and eat my greens first, everything else falls into place. I eat better and I eat less. My dietary health hinges on water and broccoli.

There's a keystone habit commended to us since the dawn of creation that may forestall *havel* in our work: sabbath keeping. The Hebrew word for sabbath, *shabbat*, means cessation. Suspension. "Six days you shall labor and do all your work," then full stop (Exodus 20:9).

That's a great act of faith. In sabbath keeping, you leave money on the table. In sabbath keeping, you set aside your preoccupation with advancing your career. While many others are out killing it (or killing themselves?), you're away from your desk, lazing about.

And who knows? Tomorrow you may arrive at work to find the world has passed you by. That's a chance you'll have to take.

But the odds are you'll hit the ground running happier and faster as your new week begins. And over the course of many weeks, you'll be healthier and more productive than those who don't have the faith to shut it down. Especially in the middle of life when energy levels dip, you'll find this well-attested, God-commanded, counterintuitive practice serving you well. In fact, it's the keystone habit behind physical and mental well-being at work.

So the corollary to the finished work of Christ is the finished work of *you*. That doesn't mean quit your job. Many of us find work demanding more of us in midlife than ever before. But like all addicts, workaholics need to know when to say when. And "when" is every seven days. Period. Full stop.

Walk Away

I (Peter) still kick myself for walking away from Laurel when she was sick. She never does that when I'm ill. So I don't want to miss the opportunity to serve her again. But beyond being more sensitive when she's ailing, I knew I needed a way to show Laurel that I was committed "in sickness and in health." I had to walk away from work more regularly for the sake of our marriage.

So I wrote my resignation letter. I addressed it to the board of directors and sealed it in an envelope. Then I told Laurel that if she felt that I was not being the husband and father she needed me to be, she could hand in my letter any time. I would walk away from the ministry I love for something I love more.

In conversations with others navigating the work-home tensions of midlife, Laurel has said something like this: "The minute you stop working at your relationship is the moment it becomes mediocre.

And mediocre stinks, making both husband and wife feel alone. It's time to get creative in growing together, especially during the craziness of raising children."

Never again am I willing to be a success at work but a failure at home. To put a twist on the Serenity Prayer, I'd rather be *reasonably happy* at work and *supremely happy* at home than the other way around. One day they'll eulogize me for my relationships, not my résumé.

(F)UTILITY

How Do We Use These Short Lives for Lasting Purposes?

You have forgotten who you are and so have forgotten me.
Look inside yourself, Simba. You are more than you have become.
You must take your place in the Circle of Life.

MUFASA, *THE LION KING*

She was giddy, shouting across the golden sand as she raced down the beach. "Daddy, come quick!" I (Peter) had just arrived with my family in Newport Beach, California, and Lili was more than a little enthusiastic. The sun was setting in a breathtaking haze of purples and golds. Not wanting to waste a second of remaining light, we hastily tossed our shoes, rolled up our jeans and sprinted into the waves.

At six the next morning, Lili was in her bathing suit and ready to go again. We were the first two people to feel the morning dew on our feet and see the foam collecting in whirlpools on the shore. Learning to surf proved far more difficult than anticipated, so in lieu of riding waves we decided to build a sandcastle.

With just a few basic tools, we built the most magnificent castle ever. It had a central fortress almost as tall as my daughter, which was guarded by thick, well-constructed walls. Every other castle ever constructed looked paltry by comparison.

As the morning wore on and my skin turned a stupid shade of tomato, I noticed the tide coming in. Lili and I had taken pains to build our castle far from the destructive waves, but apparently I underestimated the water's reach every bit as much as the sun's rays. Hours of work were under imminent threat.

As one wave washed dangerously close, Lili pleaded, "Daddy, we need to build thicker walls!" We worked furiously as the un-relenting waves lapped closer and closer. But finally a single wave breached the outer wall, causing a side of the sandcastle to col-lapse. With greater urgency, Lili shouted, "Quick, Daddy, we need to dig a moat!"

It took exactly one more wave to fill our moat to overflowing. We were no match for the mighty Pacific. Everything was reduced to short, soggy mounds. Sadly Lili sighed, "Daddy, it's all gone."

As silly as it sounds, I truly yearned to save that castle. Not that I expected it to last forever, but Lili and I had made a moment, and I wanted it to last a little longer.

What happens to castles of sand also happens to castles of steel. Our greatest works are subject to ruin. How many bulletproof business plans, ironclad deals and rock-hard bodies have melted before a wave? Fast or slow, the tide is coming in. And when it does, it will erase virtually all evidence of our ever being here.

In the immediate aftermath of our passing, someone will say something like, "Gone but not forgotten." It's a nice sentiment. But after a few more swells of everyday living, even memories of the dead fade away.

The Roman emperor Marcus Aurelius famously said, "All things fade into the storied past and in a little while are shrouded in oblivion."[1] Renowned while he was alive, Aurelius knew that even his proud achievements wouldn't be remembered after he was gone. After all, he probably couldn't recall all that much about the great Caesars who had gone before him.

So we're left with a key question to be answered in midlife, not in old age: What's the point of living if everything is dying? Can our fleeting lives leave enduring legacies?

It's Just Time Being Time

> *What do people gain from all their labors*
> *at which they toil under the sun?*
> *Generations come and generations go,*
> *but the earth remains forever.*
> *The sun rises and the sun sets,*
> *and hurries back to where it rises.*
> *The wind blows to the south*
> *and turns to the north;*
> *round and round it goes,*
> *ever returning on its course.*
> *All streams flow into the sea,*
> *yet the sea is never full.*
> *To the place the streams come from,*
> *there they return again.*
> *All things are wearisome,*
> *more than one can say.*
> *The eye never has enough of seeing,*
> *nor the ear its fill of hearing.*
> *What has been will be again,*
> *what has been done will be done again;*
> *there is nothing new under the sun.*
> *Is there anything of which one can say,*
> *"Look! This is something new"?*

It was here already, long ago;
it was here before our time.
No one remembers the former generations,
and even those yet to come
will not be remembered
by those who follow them.

ECCLESIASTES 1:3-11

For every ten people who love the cycles of nature, at least one hates them. To most people, a sunrise offers quiet moments of solitude and an inherent promise: it's a brand-new day that's never been lived before. Similarly a sunset throws a splash of color on our workday, happily ending our activities and signaling a time to rest. And tomorrow we'll get to do it all again.

But Qoheleth seems to have no such optimism. To him, a sunrise signals another day in the salt mines. A sunset grimly signals encroaching death. Its very repetitiveness is oppressive: a life of lather, rinse, repeat.

Somewhere in the vicinity of midlife we come to the place where we can relate. The rhythms that once coordinated our lives now tyrannize them. Life can feel like the same stinking things, one after the other.

Some years ago, the staff of my (Greg's) church shared our Myers-Briggs profiles on a retreat. Having recently hired several new teammates, we thought it a good idea to get to know one another using this tool. The goal was to better understand our strengths and propensities, particularly as they play out at work.

Each profile comes with a wealth of descriptors and explanations, including a short catch phrase. I (Greg) am an ENTP. The catchphrase for my type is "One adventure after another." *Bingo.* It's uncanny how accurate these things can be. The materials went on to explain that my type is the least likely of all to want to do the same thing the same way. That resonates too. Something in my very DNA craves novelty and newness. My philosophy: if it ain't broke, break it; at least you'll have a new problem to solve. Maybe I'm descended from Qoheleth and one of his thousand wives.

But here's where we get it wrong. We consider monotony akin to death and variety the essence of life. Thus we keep chasing "one adventure after another." But the old saw says that variety is the spice of life, not the substance of it.

The brilliant G. K. Chesterton saw things differently:

It is supposed that if a thing goes on repeating itself it is probably dead; a piece of clockwork. People feel that if the universe was personal it would vary; if the sun were alive it would dance. This is a fallacy even in relation to known fact. For the variation in human affairs is generally brought into them, not by life, but by death; by the dying down or breaking off of their strength or desire. A man varies his movements because of some slight element of failure or fatigue. He gets into an omnibus because he is tired of walking; or he walks because he is tired of sitting still.[2]

Hmm. Our very bodies cry for variety, not from life but from death. You shift your posture, adjust your stride or blink your eyes because of pain or discomfort. Miniature forces of death stimulate nerves that cry out for change.

But what if you had no such dark forces at work in you? Chesterton writes,

A child kicks his legs rhythmically through excess, not absence, of life. Because children have abounding vitality, because they are in spirit fierce and free, therefore they want things repeated and unchanged. They always say, "Do it again"; and the grown-up person does it again until he is nearly dead. For grown-up people are not strong enough to exult in monotony. But perhaps God is strong enough to exult in monotony. It is possible that God says every morning, "Do it again" to the sun; and every evening, "Do it again" to the moon. It may not be automatic necessity that makes all daisies alike; it may be that God makes every daisy separately, but has never got tired of making them. It may be that He has the eternal appetite of infancy; for we have sinned and grown old and our Father is younger than we. The repetition in Nature may not be a mere recurrence; it may be a theatrical *encore*.[3]

This may actually be Qoheleth's point in the opening chapter of his book.

The cycles of life are so much bigger than we are. Sun, wind and water continue to follow their courses unabated as entire generations of people pass off the scene, never to be heard from again. Our lives and works are so feeble and fleeting by comparison. In the grand scheme, Solomon's castle lasted no longer than Lili's.

The proper response to this is not despair but wonder. Qoheleth says mouths can't say enough, eyes can't see enough, ears can't hear enough. It's all too great to comprehend, and we'll wear ourselves out if we try to. The wise person will simply adjust to the reality.

The Art of Fitting into the World

Someone once said that wisdom is the art of fitting into the world. It's understanding reality and then flowing with it. It's going with the grain of the universe rather than always cutting across it.

We fit ourselves into the world as it actually is all the time. Already today you've expertly navigated it. You acknowledged the rigidity of walls and entered rooms via doors. You didn't bother trying to jump to the second floor, accepting the limits of gravity. Instead, you smartly strode up stairs, deftly lifting one foot higher than the other. You rightly considered it wisest to brew coffee with hot water and to rinse toothpaste with cold. You drove on the right side of the road, at the posted speed, honoring all traffic signs and courteously deferring to other drivers, right? (Okay, there may be limits to this illustration.)

But you get it. You've exercised wisdom and discernment in dealing with reality. Just consider the brilliant way you used paper today. You used virtually every piece properly. You blew your nose into a tissue and printed a document on twenty-pound white. You didn't attempt to buy breakfast with a sticky note or wipe your mouth with a book. These things are what they are and to try to manipulate them differently would be foolish.

Yet this is precisely what led to Solomon's frustration. Through all his considerable strengths, he was trying to make enduring marks on the world. But it was futile. The sands of time and the cycles of nature erased them all.

But what if the brevity of our lives was not an emblem of futility but a pointer to *futurity*? What if it made us look further and higher for meaning? And what if the inexorable cycles of nature didn't suggest human fruitlessness but divine faithfulness? What if they insinuated a God who always and forever carries out his purposes?

This would move us to go with the flow, to get with the program, to submit ourselves to the larger plan. In the Bible, this is called "keeping covenant," and almost nothing matters more.

One Life—You Got to Do What You Should

Now all has been heard;
here is the conclusion of the matter:
Fear God and keep his commandments,
for this is the duty of all mankind.
For God will bring every deed into judgment,

including every hidden thing,
whether it is good or evil.

ECCLESIASTES 12:13-14

Fear God and keep his commandments—that's covenant keeping, and it's "the duty of all mankind." But that's a paraphrase. The word *duty* isn't in the original text but the word *whole* is. A literal translation would be, "This is the whole of man."

This is it—the whole shooting match. There's nothing more, nothing less.

Bono once said, "Ecclesiastes is one of my favorite books. It's a book about a character who wants to find out why he's alive, why he was created. He tries knowledge. He tries wealth. He tries experience. He tries everything. You hurry to the end of the book to find out why, and it says, 'Remember your Creator.' In a way, it's such a letdown. Yet it isn't."[4] That may be the way the conclusion feels to us as well. But tease out the beauty and simplicity of this calling. All you have to do is faithfully fit yourself into this reality.

When *The Lion King* came out back in 1994, people loved the story and music, but many churchy types decried it as New Age pantheism, with its circle of life, kings ascending to the stars, a blue baboon shaman. Maybe. But looking through another set of lenses, it's almost Christian. There's creation and redemption, including a king who sacrifices his life and ascends to heaven. The creation is to be respected and stewarded, from the smallest ant to the largest antelope. Simba must take his place in the circle of life, which is symbolic of the eternal. There is a great cloud of witnesses watching from above, and now it is his turn to fulfill his holy calling during his fleeting days on earth.

It reminds me of a great Bible verse about another boy-king's earthly vocation: "When David had served God's purpose in his own generation, he fell asleep; he was buried with his ancestors and his body decayed" (Acts 13:36). That's not the most elegant summation of a life, but it's a valuable one. David served God in his day. Then he died. Then he decayed. Simple as that. From there it's on to glory, which God promises all his people will share, irrespective of the fame or anonymity of their previous lives.

It's not complicated.

Some people came to Jesus and asked, "What must we do to do the works God requires?" And Jesus answered, "The work of God is this: to believe in the one he has sent" (John 6:28-29). The people wanted to do works plural. So typical. There must be a million things God requires of us! No, Jesus says. The singular work is this: believe in me. By most classifications, that's not even a work; that's just faith.

Not that our obedience post-saved-by-grace doesn't matter. We're saved by grace apart from works in order to be sent forward into good works, as Paul said in Ephesians 2. In another passage he wrote, "To those who by persistence in doing good seek glory, honor and immortality, he will give eternal life" (Romans 2:7).

Start Passing It On Now

If we fit ourselves into the world, the fleeting nature of life will make it easier to live freely and lightly on earth. We'll live with a sense of proportion, doing the things that matter most and leaving the rest to God and others. We'll seek to give more than we receive. We'll walk in constant gratitude for this day, because future days are not guaranteed.

And when we pass, we'll pass it on. Some people lament leaving their things to others. But why not delight in it? Perhaps your daughter will take your china and remember you at holiday meals. Maybe your son will put the heirloom clock in his home, a memento to the times you spent together.

A colleague, Ashley, shared how her grandmother wanted to simplify the process—and maybe enjoy the knowledge of where her stuff would go. So she gave everyone a roll of masking tape and a marker. "Just walk around the house and put your name on the bottom of anything you'd like to have when I'm gone," she cheerfully quipped. Her family just stared, aghast. Nobody moved a muscle. Then an elated granddaughter took off running, determined to be the first to tape her name under the house!

Somebody's going to mark your stuff with his or her name. Be all right with that. But don't make too much of it, even if you're wealthy enough to leave larger legacies with your name attached.

Most of the dorms and academic buildings on our nation's campuses are named for benefactors. I (Peter) can tell you the names of the dorms where I stayed: Miller, Naugle, Kelly. But I can't tell you a thing about those people. I don't even know their gender. These folks' good names and life work became the places I bunked—and often debunked. (Note to self: if you ever build a dorm, don't skimp on the bathroom plumbing.)

But I can't knock these people, because many students had their hearts stirred, their minds stretched and their callings clarified because they went to college. They went on to build families and contribute to society in better ways than they would have otherwise. Some became presidents, and others served in places of poverty. Some built world-class companies, and others built widgets. But how many lives were enhanced—not just because they took classes, but because they got the full on-campus experience living in a dorm?

They don't need to know Miller, and Miller doesn't need to be known. God knows. And his or her legacy, like ours, is in God's hands.

The Little, Least and Last Last

Part of the adventure of living for God and not yourself is that you never know what will leave a lasting mark. But God being who he is, it probably will be something unexpected.

Whose gift became the standard for generosity? King David who dedicated his kingly fortune to the temple, or the poor, nameless woman who put two pennies in the collection?

Whose worship was more immortalized? The high priest who entered the holy of holies on the Day of Atonement to offer sacrifices on behalf of the nation, or the sinful woman who anointed Jesus' feet from her alabaster jar of perfume?

Whose faith stands as the greater model? Elijah, who called down fire from heaven, or the centurion who said to Jesus, "Just say the word, and my servant will be healed" (Matthew 8:8)?

So often it's the little things done by the littler people that leave lasting marks.

David Zac Niringiye is an Anglican bishop in Uganda and a protégé of John Stott who was educated at Wheaton College and Edinburgh. He said,

> One of the gravest threats to the North American church is the deception of power—the deception of being at the center. Those at the center tend to think, "The future belongs to us. We are the shapers of tomorrow. . . . We have a track record of success." . . . God very often is working most powerfully far from the center. Jesus is crucified outside of Jerusalem—outside—with the very cynical sign over his head, "The King of the Jews." Surprise—he is the King of the Jews. . . . Who are Jesus' brothers? The weak, the hungry, the immigrant workers, the economic outcasts. . . . Who is mostly in the company of Jesus? Not bishops and pastors! The bishops and pastors are the ones who suggest he's a lunatic! Who enjoys his company? The ordinary folk, so ordinary that their characterization is simply this: "sinners."[5]

We serve a God who does his best work at the margins. So if you find yourself working there, slogging it out through midlife, faithfully keeping covenant but subconsciously wondering if it really matters—it matters!

The last sentence of Ecclesiastes says that God will bring everything into judgment, including every hidden thing. At first hearing, that sounds threatening. Keep your nose clean! Beware your secret sins! And fair enough—those things fall into the category of "everything" that God will scrutinize. But the very last phrase of Ecclesiastes is, "whether it is good or evil." Why accentuate the negative? There may be any number of good things you've done that will be rewarded, including unknown nuggets that become legacies of pure gold in the lives of those who come after you.

Next-Gen Thinking

> *Not only was the Teacher wise, but he also imparted knowledge to the people. He pondered and searched out and set in order many proverbs. The Teacher searched to find just the right words, and what he wrote was upright and true.*

ECCLESIASTES 12:9-10

When we are no longer pursuing our own name and fame, we become free to focus on others. It's time to finally get over ourselves. Midlife is a time to transition from making it all about our accomplishments to making it about others. A time to pour into the people around us and celebrate their success. A time to share the wisdom of our first half by mentoring those younger in our second half.

Instead of sorting people by age, keeping youths, young adults and seniors in their respective stalls, what if we opened the gates and let diverse people run together? In Philip LeClerc's documentary *Divided*, he speaks about the "fifty-year failed experiment" of youth ministry. Stratifying our interactions has not served our churches or succeeding generations well.

Scott T. Brown, director of the National Center for Family Integrated Churches, said, "The church has become divided generationally. It's not doing what Scripture prescribes and is actually doing something foreign to Scripture by dividing people by age or life stage."[6]

Just as Greg helped me (Peter) navigate my thirties, I now have the privilege of trying to help a couple of younger leaders navigate theirs. It's part of the narrative arc of my story, and it's mutually beneficial. Ironically, when we stop chasing our own youth and instead pursue younger people, our passions are reenergized. If you act your age, you might feel it taking years off your soul.

Above the Sun

Human beings are role players in an epic drama. God directs, Jesus stars and we stand as townspeople in a cast of thousands. If we yearn for more stage, we'll likely be frustrated. We'll feel insignificant and trudge through our scenes with an uninspired performance. But God has made—and will make—everything beautiful in its time, including our fleeting lives and brief lines. A subplot in Jesus' climactic scene guarantees it.

One of the criminals crucified with Christ was a revolutionary against Rome. (Talk about futile work.) In many ways he typifies a wasted life, a nameless man engaged in senseless violence. But during his brief moment on stage, he said a line that goes down as one of the greatest in history: "Jesus, remember me when you come into your kingdom" (Luke 23:42).

Boom. Immortal. One moment of clarity in a life of futility, and everything changes.

We sometimes note how a legacy and reputation, carefully built over many years, can be destroyed in a moment. We in midlife do very well to remember it. But do we ever consider how a legacy and reputation can be *established* in a moment? That's a rare occurrence, to be sure. But it can happen. The anonymous thief on the cross proves it. His magnum opus, his great work, was asking to be remembered right in the moment when Rome was obliterating him. And so he became exhibit A that it's never too late to turn it around. He's the patron saint of deathbed conversions. Has anyone ever used his dying breath more wisely?

And if his life counts only because of one meaningful moment, surely yours will count for many more. Believe it. Serve God's purposes in your generation, and don't stop now just because it's grown a little humdrum or difficult. Live. Serve. Die. Decay.

Then rise forevermore.

CONCLUSION

How Do We Discover New Beginnings in Midlife?

The song I sing is a life song. Not the temporary
exuberance of youth that often fades when middle and
old age sets in with their disillusionment and cynicism. . . .
No, I'm eighty-three and I'm more excited about being
a Christian now than when I was eighteen
and I first put my feet on the way.

E. STANLEY JONES

🡵🡶

"With five pregnancies in five years, significant medical issues with two of our children and a full-time job, I was exhausted," Kim shared. "It probably shouldn't surprise me that John and I started to drift apart."

In their thirties, John took a new job based on a commission structure, with the promise of more time together. He had a strong work ethic passed down from his parents and was driven to provide for his family. Working eighty hours a week, he was physically and emotionally worn out and seemed to have little time or interest in Kim. She was taking care of their young kids in a new city and had few friends. But with many challenges at work, John had little empathy or energy to consider her needs.

Kim felt more and more isolated. "I began keeping track of the times he would even ask about my day, and it was a depressingly low number." In a conversation with her sister, Kim said, "I don't think John even loves me anymore." It was a confusing time. Her only comfort was in a young moms' Bible study, where it seemed everyone had similar struggles.

The periods of silence grew longer, and the marriage grew colder. Resentment built until any small issue made it erupt. There would be an outbreak of anger and a litany of all the things that were broken in the marriage. Then John would disappear—sometimes physically, but always emotionally. Unable to resolve the conflict, their marriage was falling apart.

Speaking from her loneliness, Kim says, "I gave up a career I loved. I was home with babies with medical needs. I was alone, with no family or deep friendships. In a fog of hurt and pain, I grew in depression and just wanted an escape."

John comments, "Our relationship was so messed up that we couldn't have a one-minute conversation without tension. I would have bet my company that our marriage was beyond repair."

Entering midlife, John and Kim's only certainty was lots of uncertainty. While the challenges mounted at home, successes and financial rewards amassed at work. "The harder I worked, the more accolades and compensation I received," John says. "Although work was my first love affair, it didn't take long before other affairs began as well." John compromised. Big-time.

There was a moment when he tried to change direction. It happened as his parents were diagnosed with cancer and then quickly passed at ages sixty-four and sixty-six. "At my father's funeral, people were lined up out the door, talking about all the wonderful things he did and what a great guy he was. I asked the question, 'What am I doing with my life?'" Like Qoheleth would say, the house of mourning was better than the house of feasting.

After the funeral, John's goal was to become more engaged with his kids and to do more good. He was even asked to be an elder at church. But trying harder wasn't working, and his life quickly slid back off the tracks.

Focusing on her kids, lonely and disconnected from John, Kim slipped into a fog. Drinking helped her sleep, and most nights she was out by the time John got home. This was not the life they had imagined.

Take a Look

Sometime around your fortieth birthday, or perhaps at the low point of your U-curve of happiness, you might receive an unusual gift: a reflective mind that soberly assesses how much satisfaction can be found under the sun. By halftime we've had enough experience to conclude, "Money isn't secure enough. Sex isn't thrilling enough. Entertainment isn't impressive enough. Music isn't interesting enough. Food isn't satisfying enough. People aren't reliable enough. This world isn't good enough."[1]

The weighty issues of life reveal a weightlessness in us, and we wonder, "Is there another way to go about this?" We humans become willing to change when the pain of change is less than the pain of staying the same.

Jesus opened the eyes of the blind, and we long to gain a new perspective like they did. To have spiritual LASIK remove the midlife blur so we can see our way clear of trivial pursuits, selfish ambitions and destructive escapes. To live for what matters most.

We want the crisis to become a gateway. We want to get a second chance to catch our second wind and start strong in the second half. We want to see if life really can begin at forty.

Part Two

In her forties and at her lowest point, Kim found herself sitting on the kitchen floor, begging God for help. Her situation was untenable, and she didn't know where to turn. Many weeks later, her life was changed by an unexpected and miraculous dream.

> In my dream, I could actually see Jesus. Not his face, but his outline. It wasn't just a presence; I knew it was him. All my senses were heightened. Then Jesus spoke three words, "Just love him."
>
> "What?" I responded. "He doesn't love me."
>
> Again, he said, "Just love him."
>
> In my dream, Jesus placed my arm on John's back, and then I felt power and a prayer flow through my arm to him. It was then that I awoke and found my arm in the exact place he had put it, despite the fact that John had not been home when I went to bed.

Knowing she had been given a directive, she began to wrestle with how it was to be done. It would require a love she didn't know. A love that was completely other-centered. A love based on a vision of Jesus and his love for her. Over the next two years, her pursuit became to love a man who didn't love her.

At various times, she struggled. It was hard! Grace is easier to show if it's reciprocated. But if grace requires reciprocation, it's not grace. Kim returned to work and became even more engaged in church, but never lost her focus on "Just love him." She knew that if she turned away from John, she would be turning away from Jesus too.

It took two years, but eventually John noticed. "Are you taking some of that feel-good medicine?" John asked after seeing the sustained change in Kim's life. It was unmistakable evidence that the Holy Spirit was at work in both of them.

A message at a church service, which John had reluctantly attended, prompted him to think about his life and eternity, and to face his brokenness. It was the first time he had ever gotten real with God. After the retreat, John headed straight to his office and wrote a letter to the woman he was involved with, saying, "I can't continue this relationship."

When he returned home that night, Kim approached him to ask directly for the first time, "Are you having an affair?"

As the details came out, Kim left for several days to mourn alone. There was so much pain, and healing would be heart-wrenchingly difficult. Yet she kept coming back to the powerful words she had heard from Christ: "Just love him." With an illogical amount of grace, the two began unpacking the lies.

John was wrecked with remorse. "There were days I couldn't even drive because I was sobbing—the I-can't-breathe type of sobbing. All this scale and mud was being removed."

For the first time, John started forming real relationships with other men. Having too much to hide, he had never allowed anyone to really know him. But after his midcourse correction, men came out of the woodwork to support him.

One in particular, Dave, became an unlikely friend. When they first met on an early Saturday morning, John watched this older man get out of his minivan and shuffle across the parking lot to the coffee shop. After making the snap judgment, "I have nothing in common with this man," John grew to respect Dave more than any other man in his life. Dave would listen intently and every once in a while ask, "Do you want to know what God says about that?" There was no condemnation; just wisdom, grace and copious amounts of love. He kept pointing John above the sun.

Kim and John went to counseling individually and eventually together. Healing wasn't instantaneous. Kim says, "It took five years for me to believe the change was real." Painful as the process was, their marriage was beautifully restored.

It's not a perfect marriage. It's not a fairy-tale life. But they're no longer chasing after the wind and reaping pain and resentment. They understand what Jesus' death and resurrection are all about. There is brokenness, but there is also beauty.

In their second act, John and Kim are not only able to love each other, they also have a new calling to help others. Their mission is simple: "Just love others as Christ has loved us." Aligning their lives with a higher purpose and a greater story, they're growing in grace and experiencing true joy.

When I (Peter) am in Houston, I stay at their home, drink their coffee, listen to their stories and learn what it means to love like Jesus.

New Vision

There is a new day dawning for John and Kim, and for those who turn their eyes to look above the sun. Jesus promised it:

> "Do not let your hearts be troubled. You believe in God; believe also in me. My Father's house has many rooms; if that were not so, would I have told you that I am going there to prepare a place for you? And if I go and prepare a place for you, I will come back and take you to be with me that you also may be where I am. You know the way to the place where I am going." (John 14:1-4)

And coming out of the grave, he proved it. Then Paul, one of the many eyewitnesses, confirmed it:

> But Christ has indeed been raised from the dead, the firstfruits of those who have fallen asleep. For since death came through a man, the resurrection of the dead comes also through a man. For as in Adam all die, so in Christ all will be made alive. But each in turn: Christ, the firstfruits; then, when he comes, those who belong to him. (1 Corinthians 15:20-23)

And even Qoheleth suspected it. He might not have foreseen Jesus' resurrection, but he knew there's a day of reckoning to come.

He also knew that through the grace of God—through an atoning sacrifice for sin—a person may find himself on God's good side in the world to come. Thus he concluded his book:

> Not only was the Teacher wise, but he also imparted knowledge to the people. He pondered and searched out and set in order many proverbs. The Teacher searched to find just the right words and what he wrote was upright and true. . . .
>
> Now all has been heard;
> here is the conclusion of the matter:
> Fear God and keep his commandments,
> for this is the duty of all mankind.
> For God will bring every deed into judgment,
> including every hidden thing,
> whether it is good or evil. (Ecclesiastes 12:9-10, 13-14)

DISCUSSION QUESTIONS

Introduction

1. Like Peter's series of near-death experiences, what moments in your life have brought you face-to-face with the brevity of life?

2. How might the shortness of life affect the way you live?

3. How have you seen your overall happiness rise and fall as you age?

4. What issues are causing you the greatest dissatisfaction?

5. Like Peter's relationship with Greg, is there someone helping you chart the waters they've already gone through? Why or why not?

1 Forty(ish)

1. What stage of life do you find yourself in? How has midlife (or its approach) affected you?

2. In the "dark wood" of midlife, what cliffs are you in danger of falling off?

3. What questions are surfacing for you at the midpoint of your life?

2 Meaning(less)

1. In what moments have you faced a sense of meaninglessness? How did you respond?

2. If this life is all that there is, how does that change your perspective on how you live it? If you have an eternal perspective, how does that affect how you live?

3. What things have you been reaching for that turned out to be just *havel*, like Greg's dog snapping at the particles of dust in the air?

3 (Dis)appointment

1. At this point in your life, what disappointments do you have with the way things have turned out this far?

2. What steps can you take to make sure that you don't find yourself on your deathbed with regrets?

3. What expectations do you have for the latter half of your life, including expectations that you may not have acknowledged consciously yet? Are these expectations realistic? Are you prepared to surrender those dreams if they don't come true?

4. What three things are you grateful for today?

4 (In)satiable

1. Has there been a moment in your life when you realized that something you had sought after didn't hold the amount of satisfaction you thought it would? How did you respond?

2. What new temptations cropped up (or intensified) as you approached or are approaching midlife?

3. Have you ever been trapped in the downward spiral of pleasure pursuit, as Greg wrote about in his Christmas Day story? What did you do? If you are trapped in one right now, what will you do?

5 (Im)mortal

1. How often do you think about the reality that you will one day die? What kinds of situations bring that reality to mind?

2. When you acknowledge your mortality, what kind of action does that prompt? What action would you like to take?

3. What would it take for you to finish well, like evangelist John R. W. Stott—with a eulogy focused on relationships?

6 (Un)charitable

1. What kind of tensions has money caused in your relationships?

2. Have you ever gotten something that you really wanted and found that it felt surprisingly empty? Why do you think that is?

3. Are you in the habit of giving? Why, or why not? How do you feel when you give?

4. Have you given others in your life the opportunity to provide feedback into your finances? Why, or why not?

7 (Un)rest

1. How do you relate to busyness? What unhealthy habits have you developed to keep up a hectic lifestyle?

2. What's at the root of your busyness? Why do you feel the need to fill up your schedule with constant activity?

3. How do you react when you consider the finite nature of our time on earth? Does it make you want to cram in as much as possible or to slow down and savor?

4. What can you eliminate from your life to give yourself margins to rest, to breathe and to listen for the Lord's voice?

8 Age(less)

1. What is the most difficult aspect of aging?

2. Have you had moments when you've been forced to realize the new limitations of your aging body? How have you responded to these changes?

3. Why do you think we are so determined to combat the natural aging process?

9 (Dis)connected

1. Think about a messy and painful relationship you've had. How has that experience affected how you relate to other people?

2. Do you feel that you have a solid community of friends? Why, or why not?

3. Who are you most prone to envy? Why? How has it impacted your relationships?

4. How have you experienced extravagant hospitality? How can you extend that same hospitality to others?

10 (Un)controllable

1. In which aspects of your life do you feel most out of control?

2. How do pain and injustice in the world make you feel about God?

3. How have you noticed your reaction to tragedy change in midlife?

4. What situations have made you recognize the limits of your control?

11 (De)humanizing

1. When have you put your work over family, relationships or your personal well-being? What made you do so?

2. Have you ever experienced physical symptoms of stress like those Ghena had? What were your symptoms?

3. What boundaries can you create to protect yourself from letting work be all-consuming?

4. Do you make time for sabbath rest? Why, or why not?

12 (F)utility

1. In what ways do you identify with Qoheleth's and Greg's frustration with the monotony of time?

2. What kind of legacy do you hope to leave behind when you die?

3. Think of three things you want to do to redeem the time you have left on earth. What specific steps will you take to accomplish these?

Conclusion

1. What does it look like to "fear God and keep his commandments," as Qoheleth instructs at the end of Ecclesiastes (12:13)?

2. What can we learn from John and Kim's story? How can we turn our lives around the same way they did?

3. Going forward, what changes do you want to make in midlife?

ACKNOWLEDGMENTS

Peter

The original title of this book was *Dead by Forty*, and there were points in the writing process when it felt like it was going to kill me. As Qoheleth said, "Much study wearies the body" (Ecclesiastes 12:12). With no other writing have I felt the support of friends and family more significantly than throughout this project.

Greg Lafferty, your sermon series started this book, but your incredible friendship finished it. Thank you for so generously giving of your time and talent to make this happen. I am deeply grateful—and I owe you big-time.

Steph Walker and Anna Haggard, you were with us from the very beginning and walked this winding road with grace and patience. Thank you.

Sarah Ann Schultz, you spent a summer researching and writing on midlife, even though it is years away for you! Thank you.

Kristine Frey, your insight, wisdom and ideas helped move this project from a draft to a book. I am so thankful for all that you do!

Chris Horst, Ashley Dickens, Jonathan Greer, Greg Gast, Jeane Miller, Bobby Parschauer and Baxter Underwood, your editing and comments made this a stronger book. Thank you.

Bob Buford, your foreword perfectly set the stage for this book and your life of service has pointed millions to look above the sun. Thank you for being a part of this book.

Derek Bell, thank you for being our connection to Halftime and enthusiastically supporting this book.

Claire Stewart, you have supported this project while simultaneously keeping everything else on track at HOPE. Thank you.

Andrew Wolgemuth, you were the first person to believe this book had potential. Thank you for being an outstanding literary agent and a friend.

Al Hsu and the InterVarsity Press team, thank you for your skill, editing and insights, which made this a much stronger book. From start to finish, working with your team has been a pleasure.

Laurel, Keith, Liliana and Myles Greer, thank you for being so patient with me as I worked on this project. Being your husband and dad is an amazing gift and the source of much joy.

Greg

I am still trying to decide if I want to thank Peter for pulling me into this. I came at it kicking and screaming from the start. But like hitting yourself in the head with a hammer, it does feel good when you stop, so thank you, Peter!

I most definitely want to thank my family for helping me to navigate midlife. My wife and kids have been wonderfully well-adjusted even when I've not been. My parents have been a model of constancy for over fifty years. And Willowdale Chapel, my spiritual family, has loved me more than I deserve. You're my all-time favorite church.

I also want to politely acknowledge age fifty for not being as bad as I thought you'd be. (But your predecessor was a punk.)

NOTES

Foreword

[1]Peter Drucker, *Managing Oneself* (Cambridge, Massachusetts: Harvard Business Press, 2007), 73.

Introduction

[1]"Life Expectancy Data by Country," Global Health Observatory Data Repository, World Health Organization, apps.who.int/gho/data/node.main .688.

[2]Jonathan Rauch, "The Real Roots of Midlife Crisis," *The Atlantic*, November 17, 2014, www.theatlantic.com/magazine/archive/2014/12/the-real-roots -of-midlife-crisis/382235.

[3]Ibid.

[4]Ibid.

[5]Jack Fallow, "Elliot Jaques: Analyzing business, the army and our midlife crises," *The Guardian*, April 11, 2003, www.theguardian.com/education /2003/apr/11/highereducation.uk1.

[6]Victor Hugo, quoted in Viv Groskop, "I'm 40: the confusion starts here," *The Guardian*, July 6, 2013, www.theguardian.com/commentisfree/2013/jul/06 /ageing-forty-birthday-groskop.

Chapter 1: Forty(ish)

[1]"Dante and the Divine Comedy: Did You Know?" *Christianity Today*, April 1, 2001, www.christianitytoday.com/ch/2001/issue70/14.2.html.

[2]"New study shows 49 percent rise in emergency department visits for drug related suicide attempts by females aged 50 and older from 2005 to

2009," SAMHSA, Newsroom, May 18, 2011, www.samhsa.gov/newsroom /press-announcements/201105181100.

[3]Sue Shellenbarger, "The Female Midlife Crisis," *Wall Street Journal*, April 7, 2005, www.wsj.com/articles/SB111283464791500330.

[4]Patricia Cohen, "In Midlife, Boomers Are Happy—and Suicidal," *New York Times*, June 12, 2010, www.nytimes.com/2010/06/13/weekinreview/13cohen .html?ref=us.

[5]Saul McLeod, "Erik Erikson," *Simply Psychology*, 2013, www.simply psychology.org/Erik-Erikson.html.

[6]Tommy Nelson, *A Life Well Lived: A Study of the Book of Ecclesiastes* (Nashville, TN: B&H Publishing Group, 2005), 35.

Chapter 2: Meaning(less)

[1]Victor Frankl, quoted in Nancy Williams, *Duty and Responsibility* (New Delhi, India: Epitome Books, 2009), 28.

[2]Daniel Ladinsky, "St. Thomas Aquinas," in *Love Poems from God: Sacred Voices from the East and West* (New York: Penguin Group, 2002), 122.

[3]Corinne Benicka, *Great Modern Masters* (New York: Excalibur Books, 1980), 130.

[4]Nicholas Brasch, *Leonardo Da Vinci: The Greatest Inventor* (New York: The Rosen Publishing Group, 2014), 7.

[5]William P. Brown, *The Seven Pillars of Creation* (Oxford, UK: Oxford University Press, 2010), 181.

[6]Nicholas Carlson, "Rich People Talk About How Happy Money Makes Them—What They Say Will Both Offend and Reassure You," *Business Insider*, December 18, 2013, www.businessinsider.com/does-being-rich-make -you-happy-2013-12.

[7]"Americans' Belief in God, Miracles and Heaven Declines," Harris, December 16, 2013, www.harrisinteractive.com/NewsRoom/HarrisPolls /tabid/447/ctl/ReadCustom%20Default/mid/1508/ArticleId/1353 /Default.aspx.

[8]Lyndall Gordon, *T. S. Eliot: An Imperfect Life* (London: Vintage, 1998), 357.

[9]C. S. Lewis, *Mere Christianity* (MacMillan, 1952), 120.

Chapter 3: (Dis)appointment

[1]"Jim Carrey: Money and Fame Are Not the Answer," *Preaching Today*,

www.preachingtoday.com/illustrations/2006/april /3040306.html.

[2]John Greenleaf Whittier, "Maud Miller" in *Mabel Martin and Other Poems* (Cambridge, MA: The Riverside Press, 1850), 38. Accessed online at www .bartleby.com/102/76.html.

[3]*We're the Millers,* directed by Rawson Marshall Thurber (New York: New Line Cinema, 2013), DVD.

[4]"Nurse reveals the top 5 regrets people make on their deathbed," *TIP News,* May 12, 2014, topinfopost.com/2014/05/12/top-5-regrets-people-make-on -their-deathbed.

[5]Garrison Keillor, "The News from Lake Wobegon," *A Prairie Home Companion*, www.prairiehome.org/listen/podcast/.

[6]Mark Buchanan, "Stuck on the Road to Emmaus: The secret to why we are not fulfilled," *Christianity Today,* July 12, 1999, www.christianitytoday.com /ct/1999/july12/9t8o55.html.

[7]Jerry Sittser, *A Grace Revealed: How God Redeems the Story of Your Life* (Grand Rapids: Zondervan, 2012), 179.

[8]C. H. Spurgeon, "The Weaned Child," delivered at Metropolitan Tabernacle, Newington, UK; text accessed at www.spurgeongems.org/vols19-21 /chs1210.pdf.

[9]Ann Voskamp, "Take the Joy Dare" (blog), *A Holy Experience*, www.aholy experience.com/joy-dares/.

[10]Sonja Lyubomirsky, *The How of Happiness: A New Approach to Getting the Life You Want* (New York: Penguin, 2008), 90.

[11]Kellie Haddock, "My Story," www.kelliehaddock.com.

Chapter 4: (In)satiable

[1]"NFL Super Bowl XLVIII Disney World Commercial with MVP Malcolm Smith Seattle Seahawks," YouTube, www.youtube.com/watch?v=11F83v JDhUA.

[2]Betsy Malloy, *The Everything Family Guide to the Disneyland Resort, California Adventure, Universal Studios and the Anaheim Area,* 2nd ed. (Avon, MA: F+W Publications, 2007), 15.

[3]For more, see Michael Budde, *The (Magic) Kingdom of God* (New York: Westview Press, 1998).

[4]Ravi Zacharias, quoted in Matt Papa, *Look and Live* (Bloomington, MN: Bethany House Publishers, 2014), 33.

[5]Personal email to Peter Greer, September 14, 2014.

[6]S. Sekles, *The Poetry of the Talmud* (New York: Published by the author, 1880), 67-68.

[7]Thomas Merton, quoted in Gordon MacDonald, *A Resilient Life* (Nashville, TN: Thomas Nelson, 2004), 150.

[8]Austin Murphy, "Staying Power," *Sports Illustrated*, January 18, 2010, www .si.com/vault/2010/01/18/105894969/staying-power.

[9]Ira Berkow, "Sports of The Times; Kerrigan Is No Bambi," *New York Times*, March 8, 1994, www.nytimes.com/1994/03/08/sports/sports-of-the-times -kerrigan-is-no-bambi.html.

[10]Reinhold Niebuhr, "The Serenity Prayer," SKDesigns, skdesigns.com /internet/articles/prose/niebuhr/serenity_prayer/.

[11]Dan Gilbert, "The Surprising Science of Happiness," TED, February 2004, www.ted.com/talks/dan_gilbert_asks_why_are_we_happy/transcript #t-156000.

[12]"The Salary That Will Make You Happy (Hint: It's Less Than $75,000)," *Forbes*, April 24, 2012, www.forbes.com/sites/learnvest/2012/04/24/the -salary-that-will-make-you-happy-hint-its-less-than-75000.

[13]Eric Barker, "6 science-based tips for making friends," *The Week*, January 28, 2014, www.theweek.com/article/index/254906/6-science-based-tips -for-making-friends.

[14]Jen Doll, "Happiness Is on a Bus to SXSW," *The Wire: News from The Atlantic*, March 9, 2012, www.thewire.com/entertainment/2012/03 /happiness-bus-sxsw/49676/.

[15]John Piper, *Desiring God* (Minneapolis, MN: Desiring God Foundation, 1986), 18.

[16]George Mueller, quoted in John Piper, "George Mueller's Strategy for Showing God," *Desiring God*, February 3, 2004, www.desiringgod.org /biographies/george-muellers-strategy-for-showing-god.

[17]Ibid.

[18]John Piper, *Seeing and Savoring Jesus Christ* (Wheaton, IL: Crossway, 2004), 15.

[19]Tony Reinke, "Trayvon, Race, and Gospel Ministry (Ask Pastor John)," *Desiring God*, July 20, 2013, www.desiringgod.org/articles/trayvon-race -and-gospel-ministry-ask-pastor-john.

Chapter 5: (Im)mortal

[1]Colin Smith, "Why Every Person Should Attend a Funeral Once a Year"

(blog), *Unlocking the Bible*, July 28, 2014, www.unlockingthebible.org
/every-person-attend-funeral-year.

[2]"The New Science of Old Age," *The Atlantic*, September 18, 2014, www
.theatlantic.com/personal/archive/2014/09/the-atlantics-october-issue
-the-new-science-of-old-age/380466/.

[3]Ernest Becker, *The Denial of Death* (New York: Simon & Schuster, 1973),
283.

[4]Ibid., 283-84.

[5]Samuel Johnson, quoted in George Sim Johnston, "A Melancholy Man of
Letters," *Wall Street Journal*, September 18, 2008, www.wsj.com/articles
/SB122169595583050185.

[6]Ed Pilkington, "Survivors of the Hudson River plane crash," *The Guardian*,
February 4, 2010, www.theguardian.com/world/2010/feb/04/survivors
-hudson-river-plane-crash.

[7]Becker, *Denial of Death*, 196.

[8]Sia, "Chandelier" from *1000 Forms of Fear*, RCA Records/Inertia Records,
released July 4, 2014, www.azlyrics.com/lyrics/sia/chandelier.html.

[9]Mario D. Garrett, "Faith Leaders and End-of-Life," *Psychology Today*, September 29, 2013, www.psychologytoday.com/blog/iage/201309/faith-leaders
-and-end-life.

[10]See David Brooks's TED Talk, www.ted.com/talks/david_brooks_should
_you_live_for_your_resume_or_your_eulogy?language=en.

[11]Chris Norton, "Leaders and Friends Remember Stott," *Christianity Today*,
July 29, 2011, www.christianitytoday.com/ct/2011/julyweb-only/johnstott
roundup.html?start=1.

[12]Michael Jensen, "Christ Abolished Death: John Stott (1921–2011)," *Religion
and Ethics*, August 4, 2011, www.abc.net.au/religion/articles/2011/08/01
/3283028.htm.

[13]Norton, "Leaders and Friends Remember Stott."

[14]Rob Moll, *The Art of Dying* (Downers Grove, IL: InterVarsity Press, 2010),
83.

Chapter 6: (Un)charitable

[1]Sonya Britt, "Divorce Study: Financial Arguments Early in Relationship
May Predict Divorce," *Huffington Post*, July 16, 2013, www.huffingtonpost
.com/2013/07/12/divorce-study_n_3587811.html.

[2]"10 Ideas That Are Changing Your Life," *TIME*, March 12, 2012, content

.time.com/time/magazine/article/0,9171,2108054,00.html.

[3]Todd Harper, "Discipling Affluent Christians into Generous Givers," *Generous Giving*, May 15, 2003, library.generousgiving.org/articles/display .asp?id=118.

[4]Les Christie, "America's Homes Are Bigger Than Ever," *CNN Money*, June 5, 2014, http://money.cnn.com/2014/06/04/real_estate/american-home-size.

[5]Compare "Statistics and Facts About Car Drivers" (The Statistics Portal, www.statista.com/topics/1197/car-drivers) and "253 Million Cars and Trucks on U.S. Roads" (*LA Times*, June 9, 2014, www.latimes.com/business/autos /la-fi-hy-ihs-automotive-average-age-car-20140609-story.html).

[6]Dean Schabner, "Americans Work More than Anyone," *ABC News*, May 1, 2014, http://abcnews.go.com/US/story?id=93364&page=1.

[7]Patrick Clark, "Hoarder Nation: America's Self-Storage Industry is Booming," *Bloomberg Business*, December 1, 2014, www.bloomberg.com/bw/articles /2014-12-01/cyber-monday-gifts-final-resting-place-self-storage.

[8]Katie Hetter, "Get happy in the world's happiest countries," *CNN*, March 21, 2014, www.cnn.com/2014/03/20/travel/happiest-countries-to-visit/.

[9]Dennis Okholm, *Dangerous Passions, Deadly Sins: Learning from the Psychology of Ancient Monks* (Grand Rapids: Brazos Press, 2014), 76.

[10]Ibid, 83.

[11]Ted Allrich, "How Much Money Is Enough?" *Nasdaq*, August 27, 2010, www.nasdaq.com/article/how-much-money-is-enough-cm34225.

[12]"GDP per capita (current US$)," The World Bank, data.worldbank.org /indicator/NY.GDP.PCAP.CD.

[13]"Congo, Dem. Rep.," The World Bank, data.worldbank.org/country/congo -dem-rep.

[14]United Nations, "Congo (Democratic Republic of the)," *Human Development Report 2013*, hdr.undp.org/sites/default/files/Country-Profiles/ COD.pdf.

[15]Frank Greve, "America's poor are its most generous givers," *McClatchyDC*, May 19, 2009, www.mcclatchydc.com/2009/05/19/68456/americas-poor -are-its-most-generous.html.

[16]Al Hsu, email to Peter Greer, September 30, 2014.

[17]Lalin Anik, et al., *Feeling Good About Giving: The Benefits (and Costs) of Self-Interested Charitable Behavior* (Boston: Harvard Business School Working Paper, 2009), 10.

[18]Ibid.

[19]Robert Putnam, *Bowling Alone: The Collapse and Revival of American Community* (New York: Simon & Schuster, 2000), 123.

Chapter 7: (Un)rest

[1]Jason Cranfordteague, "Digiphrenia—Excerpt from Douglas Rushkoff's *Present Shock*," *WIRED*, March 26, 2013, archive.wired.com/geekdad/2013/03/digiphrenia-excerpt-from-douglas-rushkoffs-present-shock/.

[2]Camille Peri, "Coping with Excessive Sleepiness: 10 Things to Hate About Sleep Loss," *WebMD*, February 13, 2014, www.webmd.com/sleep-disorders/excessive-sleepiness-10/10-results-sleep-loss?page=3.

[3]Dennis Okholm, *Dangerous Passions, Deadly Sins: Learning from the Psychology of Ancient Monks* (Grand Rapids: Brazos Press, 2014), 135.

[4]Sheldon Vanauken, *A Severe Mercy* (New York: HarperCollins, 2011), 200.

[5]Ibid.

[6]Ibid.

[7]Ibid., 201.

[8]John Ortberg, "Ruthlessly Eliminate Hurry," *Leadership Journal*, July 4, 2002, www.christianitytoday.com/le/2002/july-online-only/cln20704.html.

[9]Blaise Pascal, *Pensées*, trans. A. J. Krailscheimer (London: Penguin, 1966), no. 136.

[10]Douglas Rushkoff, *Present Shock: When Everything Happens Now* (Douglas Rushkoff, 2013), 2.

[11]J.D. Greear, "A Tool for Saturating Yourself in the Gospel Daily," J.D. Greear, May 28, 2011, www.jdgreear.com/my_weblog/2011/05/a-tool-for-saturating-yourself-in-the-gospel-daily.html.

[12]"Warren Buffet, quoted in "Are You Focused Enough? (A Surprising Case Study)," *Forbes*, May 10, 2012, www.forbes.com/sites/actiontrumpseverything/2012/05/10/are-you-focused-enough-a-surprising-case-study.

Chapter 8: Age(less)

[1]Jen Hatmaker, Facebook post, December 30, 2014, 6:37 p.m., www.facebook.com/pages/Jen-Hatmaker/203920953040241?fref=photo.

[2]Ethan Huff, "The United States of plastic surgery: Americans spent $11 billion last year on facelifts, Botox, breast augmentations," *Natural News*, May 2, 2013, www.naturalnews.com/040164_plastic_surgery_breast_augmentation_Botox.html.

[3]"Annual AAFPRS Survey Finds 'Selfie' Trend Increases Demand for Facial

Plastic Surgery Influence on Elective Surgery," American Academy of Facial Plastic and Reconstructive Surgery, March 11, 2014, www.aafprs .org/media/stats_polls/m_stats.html.

[4]Jennifer Weiner, "Great! Another Thing to Hate About Ourselves," *New York Times*, February 14, 2015, http://www.nytimes.com/2015/02/15/opinion /sunday/from-sports-illustrated-the-latest-body-part-for-women-to-fix .html?_r=0.

[5]Vivian Diller, "Too Young to Look Old: What Youth Fears About Aging," *Psychology Today*, February 8, 2011, https://www.psychologytoday.com /blog/face-it/201102/too-young-look-old-what-youth-fears-about-aging.

[6]Cameron Russell, "Looks aren't everything. Believe me, I'm a model," *TED*, October 2012, www.ted.com/talks/cameron_russell_looks_aren_t _everything_believe_me_i_m_a_model/transcript.

[7]"7 Cultures That Celebrate Aging and Respect Their Elders," *Huffington Post*, February 25, 2014, www.huffingtonpost.com/2014/02/25/what-other -cultures-can-teach_n_4834228.html.

[8]Dan Buettner, "How to Live to Be 100+," *TED*, September 2009, www.ted .com/talks/dan_buettner_how_to_live_to_be_100?language=en.

[9]Paulina Porizkova, "Aging," *Huffington Post*, October 21, 2010, www .huffingtonpost.com/paulina-porizkova/aging_b_771127.html.

[10] Rodney Sauder, conversation with Peter Greer, January 10, 2015.

[11]"The Aging Brain," Brain Institute at Oregon Health and Science University, www.ohsu.edu/xd/health/services/brain/in-community/brain-awareness /brain-health/aging-brain.cfm.

[12]See "Research in Sitting & Standing," JustStand.org, www.juststand.org /tabid/636/language/en-US/default.aspx.

[13]Kent Annan, "How the Tough Mudder Shaped My Soul," *Christianity Today*, June 25, 2014, www.christianitytoday.com/ct/2014/june/how-doing -tough-mudder-shaped-my-soul.html?share=wCZYRMuw+iwOXN /9x8YloF5QHAZsq/Et&start=1.

Chapter 9: (Dis)connected

[1]*About a Boy*, directed by Chris Weitz and Paul Weitz (Universal City, CA: Universal Pictures, 2002), DVD.

[2]Jessica Olien, "Loneliness Is Deadly," *Slate*, August 23, 2013.

[3]Al Hsu, personal email to Peter Greer, December 30, 2014.

[4]We are not bashing Facebook or social media. There are wonderful up-sides to it. But it's insufficient for deep friendship, as many can attest.

[5]*The Invention of Lying*, directed by Ricky Gervais and Matthew Robinson (Burbank, CA: Warner Home Video, 2010), DVD.

[6]Brené Brown, "The Power of Vulnerability," TED, June 2010, www.ted.com /talks/brene_brown_on_vulnerability?language=en.

[7]M. Scott Peck, *The Different Drum: Community Making and Peace* (New York: Touchstone, 1987), 106.

[8]Rodney Stark, *The Rise of Christianity: How the Obscure, Marginal Jesus Movement Became the Dominant Religious Force in the Western World in a Few Centuries* (New York: HarperCollins, 1996), 114.

[9]Ibid., 83.

[10]Kristi Black, "40th Birthday Random Acts of Kindness" (blog), *Kristi's Chaos*, January 24, 2013, kristischaos.com/2013/07/24/40th-birthday -random-acts-of-kindness/.

Chapter 10: (Un)controllable

[1]Joseph Shapiro, "Amish Forgive School Shooter, Struggle with Grief," *NPR*, October 2, 2007, www.npr.org/templates/story/story.php?storyId=14900930.

[2]Leo G. Perdue, *Scribes, Sages and Seers: The Sage in the Eastern Mediterranean World* (Göttingen, Germany: Vandenhoeck & Reprecht, 2009), 203.

[3]Jerry Sittser, *A Grace Disguised* (Grand Rapids: Zondervan, 1995), 64.

[4]Ibid., 110-11.

[5]Ann Patchett, "Scared Senseless," *New York Times Magazine*, October 20, 2002, www.nytimes.com/2002/10/20/magazine/20WWLN.html.

[6]Sittser, *A Grace Disguised*, 202-3.

Chapter 11: (De)humanizing

[1]Patrick J. Skerrett, "Is retirement good for health or bad for it?" *Harvard Health Publications*, December 10, 2012, www.health.harvard.edu/blog /is-retirement-good-for-health-or-bad-for-it-201212105625.

[2]Paige Baschuk, *The Advisory Board Company*, May 16, 2013, www.advisory .com/daily-briefing/blog/2013/05/retirement-causes-a-drastic-decline-in -health-study-says.

[3]Gordon MacDonald, *A Resilient Life* (Nashville, TN: Thomas Nelson, 2004), 88.

Chapter 12: (F)utility

[1]Robert Bonser, *Facing Our Mortality Without Fear: Advice from the Great Philosophers* (Bloomington, IN: iUniverse, 2011), 21.

[2]G. K. Chesterton, *Orthodoxy* (Rockville, MD: Serenity), 52.

[3]Ibid, 108-9.

[4]Bono, quoted in Denis Haack, "Johnny Cash: Clouded by Sin, Colored by Grace," *byFaith*, July/August 2005, 39.

[5]David Zac Niringiye, quoted in Andy Crouch, "Experiencing Life at the Margins: An African Bishop Tells North American Christians the Most Helpful Gospel-Thing They Can Do," *Christianity Today*, July 1, 2006, www.christianitytoday.com/ct/2006/july/31.32.html.

[6]Alex Murshako, "Modern Youth Ministry a '50-Year Failed Experiment,' Say Pastors," *Christian Post*, July 28, 2011, www.christianpost.com/news/church-services-separated-by-age-un-biblical-say-former-youth-pastors-52964/.

Conclusion

[1]Matt Papa, *Look and Live* (Bloomington, MN: Bethany House, 2014), 33.

ABOUT THE AUTHORS

Peter Greer

Peter is president and CEO of HOPE International, a global, Christ-centered microfinance organization serving throughout Africa, Asia, Latin America and Eastern Europe.

He is a graduate of Messiah College (BS, 1997), Harvard's Kennedy School (MPP, 2004) and Erskine College (honorary PhD, 2012).

Internationally, Peter served as a microfinance adviser in Cambodia, technical adviser for Self-Help Development Foundation in Zimbabwe and managing director for Urwego in Rwanda.

As an advocate for the church's role in missions and alleviating extreme poverty, Peter has been a featured speaker at conferences such as Catalyst, Passion, Harvard International's Development Conference and Jubilee, and he has been featured in *Christianity Today*, *World*, *Forbes*, *Relevant* and *Outcomes Magazine*, and on CNN.

Peter has written *The Poor Will Be Glad* (2009, with Phil Smith), *The Spiritual Danger of Doing Good* (2013, with Anna Haggard), *Mission Drift* (2014, with Chris Horst), *Entrepreneurship for Human Flourishing* (2014, with Chris Horst), *The Giver and the Gift* (2015, with David Weekley) and *Watching Seeds Grow* (2014, with his son Keith).

Peter and Laurel, his wife, live in Lancaster, Pennsylvania, with their three children.

Learn more at peterkgreer.com; Facebook: peterkgreer; Twitter: @peterkgreer.

To contact Peter for a speaking request or to subscribe to his blog, please visit peterkgreer.com.

Greg Lafferty

Greg Lafferty is the senior pastor of Willowdale Chapel, a church with campuses in Kennett Square and Jennersville, Pennsylvania. A 1984 graduate of Wheaton College, he cut his ministry teeth working with junior high kids for ten years before they finally let him hang around with adults.

Previously Greg served at both Wheaton Bible Church and Christ Community Church in suburban Chicago, and Saddleback Church in Southern California. Greg's boyhood dream was to succeed Brooks Robinson at third base for the Baltimore Orioles. Or to be a pastor. Thank God for Plan Bs.

He's been blessed to serve the church his entire vocational career and to do so alongside his wife of over thirty years, Deane.

When not overly consumed by his job, Greg likes to work out, read a book, see a movie or tackle the *New York Times* crossword puzzle.

The Laffertys have three young adult children, Kelsey, Krista and Ryan. Kelsey is studying graduate-level math at Purdue, Krista is studying communications at Northwestern and Ryan is studying the DMV driver's manual at home. They are immense sources of joy and blessing.